SACRED HEART ACADEMY

125 Years Of Excellence In Education Rooted In Ursuline Tradition

SACRED HEART ACADEMY

125 Years Of Excellence In Education Rooted In Ursuline Tradition

URSULINE CAMPUS SCHOOLS

Sponsored by the Ursuline Sisters

SHA 125

EXCELLENCE IN EDUCATION
ROOTED IN URSULINE TRADITION

Front cover: Sacred Heart Academy Graduate, 1923
Back cover: Graduates, 2002
Endsheets: Graduates, 1912

CONTENTS

TAPROOTS
The Ursuline Sisters   14

HEARTWOOD
Sacred Heart Academy   32

BRANCHING OUT
Academics   86

STRONG LIMBS
Athletics   114

SHELTERING CANOPY
Christian Foundation   154

TENDING NEW SHOOTS
Faculty   172

TAKING A BOUGH
Arts   194

PRESSED FLOWERS
Traditions   216

HEARTY BRANCHES
Other Campus Schools   248

SOWING SEEDS
The Future   270

ACKNOWLEDGMENTS   283

TIMELINE
Sacred Heart Academy's Place
In History: 1877-2002   285

To the Ursuline Sisters, who have educated and
inspired generations of women to strive for excellence,
to fulfill their dreams, and to lead lives of service
to God and to others. Their love and support have
taught us the true meaning of education.

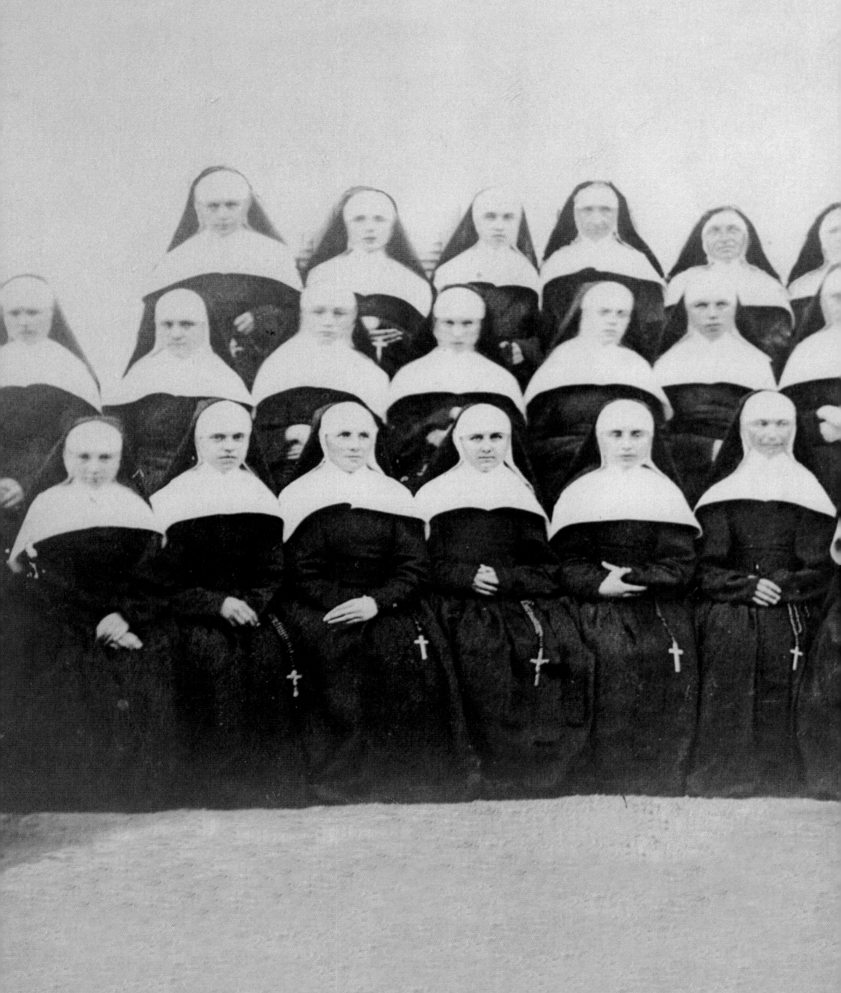

TAPROOTS
The Ursuline Sisters

TAPROOTS

The Ursuline Sisters

by Dianne Aprile '67

For us you've striven, to us you've given

Getting there was not half the fun. Getting there, in truth, was no fun.

The ship they intended to sail, the *Austria*, caught fire at sea before it ever reached port for them to board, a calamity that resulted in the deaths of all its passengers. The *Ariel*, the ship they ultimately sailed on in its stead, had twice before come close to disaster at sea. Now, on their long journey across the Atlantic, the *Ariel* seemed as ill-starred as ever. The first mishap, an on-board explosion, was followed by yet another close call when a Turkish man-of-war rammed her broadside as she hauled into New York Harbor on October 23, 1858.

The three Ursuline Sisters who rode the ship from Bremen, Germany, to New York Harbor couldn't have imagined a more harrowing trip. Who knows what strong emotions occupied their hearts as they touched dry land—more than a month after their departure from Straubing, Bavaria. They were now, officially, German immigrants to the United States.

At the start of their journey, Sister Salesia Reitmeier, the trio's young but capable leader, was given 85 Deutschemarks when she left the convent on September 13. That was the equivalent of $22.50 in U.S. currency, small change even in those days. Though they were uncertain of their finances, the sisters had no doubts about their mission: to build a new home in Louisville, Kentucky, a port city on

the Ohio River, where the children of German-Catholic immigrants were in dire need of education and religious instruction.

The $22.50 they carried with them from Straubing was intended to cover their expenses while traveling. The voyage itself was financed by a missionary society, the Ludwigs-Missionsverein. Upon their arrival in Louisville, the close-knit immigrant community opened its arms and heart to the sisters. The German-Americans of Saint Martin parish, in particular, needed the sisters' services and were eager to help them get started.

That had been the plan outlined by Father Leander Streber, O.F.M. of Louisville, when he visited Saint Ursula Convent in Straubing earlier that summer. At the request of Bishop Martin John Spalding of Louisville, Streber—a sacristan at Louisville's Cathedral of the Assumption before his ordination—pleaded for assistance from the Bavarian Ursulines. Streber, according to reports at the time, met Sister Salesia when she was a child in Straubing and he a Franciscan Friar; he predicted at that time that she would someday join him in a foreign mission.

Meeting the contemporary needs of Catholics, particularly the educational needs of the young, was at the heart of the Ursuline way of life. Still, Sister Salesia's superiors in the convent and diocese did not

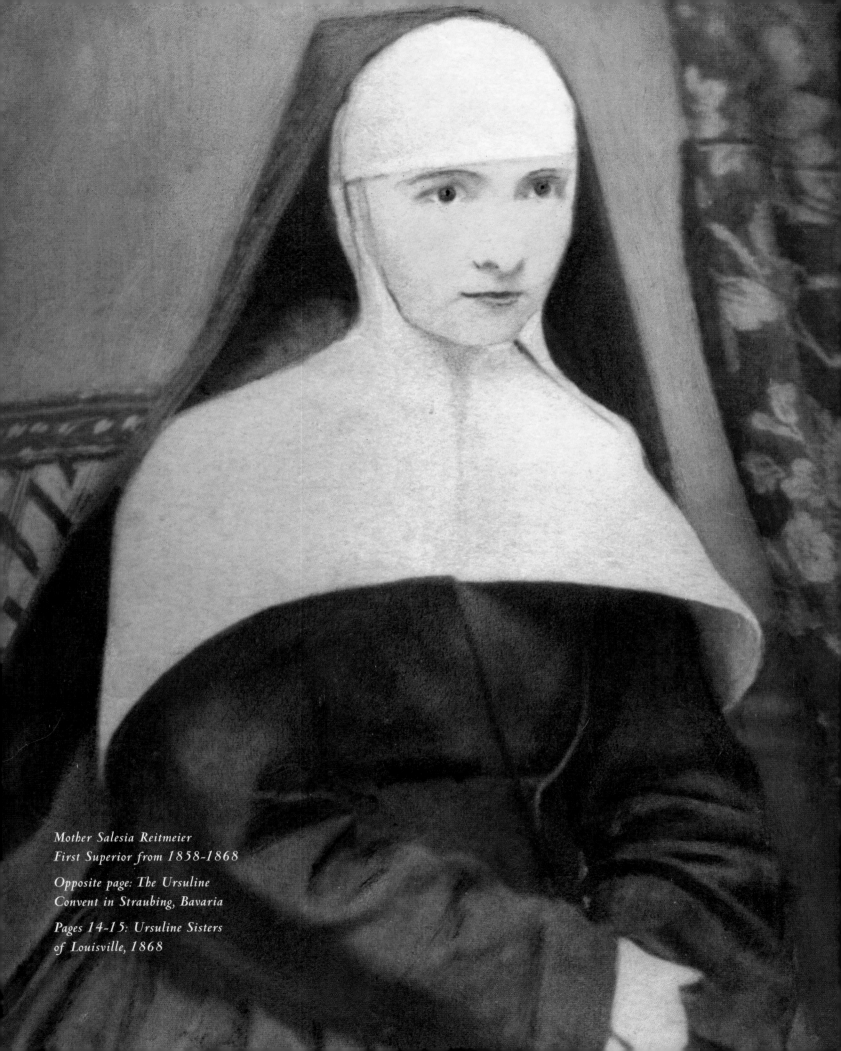

Mother Salesia Reitmeier
First Superior from 1858-1868

Opposite page: The Ursuline
Convent in Straubing, Bavaria

Pages 14-15: Ursuline Sisters
of Louisville, 1868

Above: Sister Pia Schoenhofer

Left: Sister M. Maximillian Zwinger

Below: Ursuline's first convent in Louisville, 1858 (photo, 1940)

Opposite page: Ursuline Academy, 1860

want to let her go. Many years later, Mother Pia explained their reluctance this way: "The proposition was so uncommon, so new, so strange, the land so unknown, the chances for success so gloomy and uncertain." Add to that Sister Salesia's talents, so useful to her own community: she spoke French as well as German, played piano and guitar, sang and sewed beautifully. Her only weakness seemed to be constitutional—she was a woman of delicate frame and fragile health.

Even her family insisted she stay put in her homeland, vowing to cut off all contact with her if she left for America. But Sister Salesia was resolute, and her superiors relented. With Sisters Pia and Maximillian, both volunteers, she sailed for the New World, a place none of them, it can be safely assumed, ever dreamed of seeing.

Now, in New York Harbor, they placed themselves in the hands of the Dominican Sisters of Brooklyn, who generously welcomed them into their convent for rest and rejuvenation after the long, exhausting trip. Three days later, on October 26, the sisters, with Father Streber, resumed their journey by train to Cincinnati, then by steamboat to Louisville.

They arrived October 31, 1858, the eve of All Saints Day. They quietly moved into their first home in Louisville, a modest frame house on Campbell Street, consisting of two rooms and a garret. From one of the windows, the view opened up to a nearby lot on Chestnut Street already earmarked as the site for their first convent and boarding school.

Their new home was humble; their neighborhood urban, immigrant, quintessentially American—unlike any place they had ever lived, or even visited. Changes they could not fathom lay in wait for them. Together, however, they would find security in their faith, comfort in their centuries-old spiritual practices and inspiration in the overwhelming needs of the community they were committed to serve.

And certainly they found solace in one another. They were three determined women, two very young and one middle-aged: Sister Salesia Reitmeier and Sister Pia Schoenhofer were both 26; Sister Maximillian Zwinger, 50.

The three Ursulines had no way of knowing, of course, that their journey would become the essential

Saint Angela Merici
(c. 1470-1540)
Founder of the
Ursuline Sisters

Opposite page:
Desenzano, Italy

link between the great life and work of Saint Angela Merici in 16th century Italy and the education of 21st century young women at Sacred Heart Academy in Louisville, Kentucky.

Books and scholarly papers by Ursuline historians have touched on this brief moment in time, when three nuns left the Old World to set up shop, as it were, an ocean and more than a few culture-shocks away. They arrived three years before the U.S. Civil War began, when food was scarce, slavery was legal and women were a long way from getting the vote. Along with their rosaries and prayer books, they brought a proud tradition of female courage and independence. They may have come to Louisville at the request of a man, but it was a woman, their superior, Mother Josepha, who permitted them to make the journey. Far from home, they faced every sort of obstacle but never turned back, never gave up, never lost faith.

Sister Helen Margaret Schweri, a Louisville Ursuline author, has drawn interesting comparisons between the lives of Saint Angela, the founder of the Ursulines, and Sister Salesia, the 26-year-old Ursuline Sister who was charged with founding and supervising the convent in Louisville. Mother Salesia (whose baptismal name, coincidentally, was Ursula) grew up in the Bavarian village of Heidfling, one of six children, four of whom died as infants. She enrolled in the convent boarding school at Straubing at the age of 12, went on to enter the Ursuline novitiate there and, at age 21, made her vows.

Unlike Saint Angela, who from an early age traveled widely and confidently in intellectual, sophisticated circles, Sister Salesia had lived a cloistered life—in every sense—from her childhood until the day she stepped aboard the *Ariel*. Angela lived nearly 70 years. Sister Salesia was dead at 36. Yet, as the author points out in her book, *Under His Mighty Power*, the common bond between the two women was an unshakable faith and genuine willingness to serve God's world— to meet the needs of the time.

Sister Salesia's eagerness to take on a job outside her scope of experience is understood best in the context of Saint Angela's extraordinary life and unprecedented work.

Angela Merici was born sometime between 1470 and 1474. Like so many of the details of this Renaissance woman's life, the exact year of her birth is not recorded. We do know she was born in Desenzano, a village in northern Italy, and that over the course of her life, she lived in several towns in the region. The best-known of these towns were Saló, where she became a member of the Third Order Franciscans, and Brescia, where she died in a room attached to the Church of Saint Afra, later renamed for her.

Angela's father, Giovanni, was a peasant farmer, but his wife had relatives who were wealthy and well-connected in Italian society. Though Angela never learned to write, her father taught her to read. Throughout her adult life, she "wrote" by dictating to a secretary, or *amanuensis*, a common practice of the time.

The incident that biographers point to as the organizing event of Angela's youth, the milestone that guided her to a path of spiritual commitment and service to others, occurred in her early adolescence. Angela had lost her beloved sister and, in her grief, was inspired to pray daily for a sign of her sister's union with God. Ultimately these prayers led to a religious experience—a vision—which included hearing a call from God to establish a company of consecrated virgins. It would be many years later, when Angela was in her 60s, that the calling would be fulfilled.

As a member of the Third Order Franciscans, Angela was sent on a mission to Brescia to take care of the widow, Catherine Patengola. While in Brescia, a city devastated by war and corruption, she was affiliated with a group of young men and women who

devoted themselves to nursing the sick and protecting vulnerable children. She was, by all accounts, a good listener and an insightful adviser.

Today the Ursuline Sisters see Angela's primary gift, or charism, to be that of a counselor and reconciler, one whom people trusted, confided in and relied upon for wisdom in complicated matters.

In 1535, after pilgrimages to holy places in Italy, and following another profound religious experience, Angela fulfilled her calling by forming the Company of Saint Ursula, named for the fourth century patron saint of young people. What was fundamentally different about her Company was that Angela clearly did not intend for it to be an order of cloistered nuns, like the Poor Clares or Benedictines. Simply put, it was a group of women, remaining "in the world," who were called to live a holy life in service to their neighbors. They did not live in a convent but rather with their families or at their workplaces. Angela dictated her own Rule, which won approval from the Vicar of her diocese, and offered a way of life for women that was unprecedented at that time.

However, at Angela's death in 1540, the Company's unorthodox dress and living arrangements came under fire. Ten years after she died, many groups that were affiliated with the Company abandoned her Rule and philosophy of "living in the world" and accepted in its place a monastic rule requiring a life of seclusion and adoption of a religious habit. These cloistered groups became known as the Order of Saint Ursula, or Ursulines, and spread quickly throughout Italy.

Today, Ursulines have ministries all over the world, while Angelines, followers of Angela whose leaders never accepted monasticism, live and work primarily in northern Italy. Other groups of men and women are also affiliated with the Ursulines in a variety of formal and informal associations.

By 1691, Ursulines had also established convents in France and Germany. One hundred years later, at the time of the French Revolution, there were more Ursulines than any other single order in France. Nine thousand Ursulines were teaching in 350 girls' schools, all of whose students were deprived of an education during the post-Revolution suppression of religious orders in Europe.

Among the convents taken over by the government in that era was Saint Ursula Kloster in Straubing. In the midst of this turmoil, in 1807, Angela Merici was canonized. In 1828, the convent in Bavaria reopened and over the next few decades grew and prospered.

Fifty years after Angela's official sainthood, and no doubt inspired by it, Sisters Salesia, Pia and Maximillian left their beloved motherhouse for what must surely have seemed like the wilds of Louisville, Kentucky.

Once settled in Louisville, the fledgling Ursuline community quickly got to work. In short order, with Sister Pia in charge of academic matters, the sisters opened a grade school for girls, a high school that took boarders, a training school for teachers and a novitiate for sisters in training. Construction of new buildings and classrooms kept everyone busy. By 1864, "The Ursuline Society and Academy of Education" was legally incorporated by the Kentucky state legislature.

Meanwhile, Mother Salesia dedicated herself to the construction of a chapel at the corner of Shelby and Chestnut streets. "A convent without a church is only halfwork," she told her sisters. Yet, she did not live to see its completion. The disastrous collapse of a wall delayed the project considerably. Then, an illness triggered by the shock of the accident proved too much for Mother Salesia. The founder and first Mother Superior of the Louisville Ursulines died on June 25, 1868, six months before the chapel was dedicated. At the time of her death, the motherhouse had become home to 41 sisters, novices and postulants —a twelve-fold increase in just ten years.

Mother Salesia's successor, Mother Martina Nicklas, was a young nun from Germany who had come to

Mother M. Martina Nicklas,
Second Superior
from 1868-1881

Opposite page: Brescia, Italy

Louisville in 1860 expressly to enter the Ursuline order. During her time as leader of the community, the sisters continued to expand their influence and service to other parts of Kentucky and to Maryland, Indiana and Illinois.

Most notably, in 1877 Mother Martina purchased land on Shelbyville Branch Turnpike, now known as Lexington Road. Situated only a few miles east of the motherhouse, the land was considered a "country estate" in those days. Under Sister Martina's leadership, the Ursulines opened a school for grades one through twelve in a three-story mansion on the estate.

The sisters named the school the Academy of the Sacred Heart.

In 1881, with Sacred Heart already off to a solid start and the Ursuline community now standing at 108 members, Mother Pia was elected its third superior. She was one of the founding three Ursulines and had taught several years at a new school in Daviess County called Mount Saint Joseph Academy. The Ursulines by this time were in charge of 20 schools.

In 1884, Mother Pia's term ended and she chose to return to the convent in Straubing, where she died 33 years later.

With her departure, all direct links between Straubing and Louisville ended. Yet the pioneering spirit of the three founding sisters and their generous motherhouse in Bavaria was as strong as ever in Louisville.

The Ursulines put down deep roots, from which they spread the legacy of Saint Angela to all ends of

the city, branching into the rural areas of Kentucky and crossing state borders. In 2002, Ursulines of Louisville minister in Kentucky, Maryland, Mississippi, Iowa, California, Indiana, West Virginia, South Carolina, Nebraska, Ohio, Pennsylvania and Peru, South America.

But the Lexington Road campus, home to the motherhouse and the setting for so much of the sisters' extraordinary history, is especially dear to the hearts of the Ursuline Sisters. And it is Sacred Heart Academy—the first school to blossom on that beautiful, secluded, tree-shaded campus—that stands as a reminder of the remarkable vision of their founder, Saint Angela Merici, and her followers.

For those of us with ties to Sacred Heart Academy, her history is our history. From Brescia to Bavaria. From Chestnut Street to Lexington Road. Like a tree in spring, unfurling its foliage leaf by leaf, Sacred Heart's history unfolds in the chapters that follow— page after page, memory by memory.

"Have each and every one engraved within your heart, for real love acts and works this way."

—Saint Angela Merici

The charism of Angela and the charism of the Ursuline Sisters of Louisville is a contemplative love of God and a resulting openness and eagerness to serve the needs of others.

"*Live and behave in such a way that others may see themselves mirrored in you.*"

—Saint Angela Merici

HEARTWOOD

Sacred Heart Academy

HEARTWOOD

Sacred Heart Academy

by Dianne Aprile '67

Dear Sacred Heart, school of my heart

It did not take long for the Ursuline Sisters of Louisville to realize their bold dream of a new school "in the country." Within two decades of their emigration from Germany, the community opened the Academy of the Sacred Heart. Under the direction of Sister Florence Meder, the new school began life in a three-story brick mansion located on what is now known as Lexington Road.

The mansion, which was part of the wooded estate when the sisters purchased it on August 1, 1877, became home to Sacred Heart's first five students when it opened its doors that October. At first, only day students from the neighborhood were accepted for admission; later boarders joined the class ranks. To accommodate the growing enrollment, a two-story wing was added to the mansion in two separate installments. By 1887, Ursuline Academy on East Chestnut Street had become strictly a day school, and SHA enrolled only boarding students.

At the turn of the century, despite the additions, it became clear that Sacred Heart needed a new building. Not only were there too many students to squeeze into the building, but in 1894, the Ursuline Sisters had moved their novitiate to the "country campus," too.

In 1903, the cornerstone was laid for a new home for Sacred Heart Academy, a building designed by the architect C. A. Curtin.

The novitiate took over the mansion when the new school opened. But the new Sacred Heart building was short-lived; it was destroyed by fire in the spring of 1918.

The cause of the fire was never officially determined. Fortunately, no one was seriously hurt, and classes were disrupted for only two weeks. Until the second new school building opened in 1926, classes were conducted and boarders housed in the recently completed motherhouse.

Despite its isolation from the bustle of the city, Sacred Heart seemed forever in the midst of change. In 1937, during the Great Ohio River Flood, the campus housed refugees. In 1938, Ursuline College—which had opened in 1921 as Sacred Heart Junior College—began offering four-year degrees. In 1940, a year clouded by war, Sacred Heart graduated its last boarding student and became strictly a day school.

In the mid-1950s, historic Angela Hall—the original campus mansion and home to both the Academy and the Model School—was torn down. On its site, Marian Hall was built as a residence hall for the college. A new Angela Hall was constructed on the east side of campus to house Sacred Heart Model School.

In 1963, having by then outgrown its 40-year-old "new building," Sacred Heart Academy moved again—this time to its present location at the northeast edge

*Eva J. Walter,
Graduation, 1906*

*Opposite page:
Mother Florence Meder,
first director of Sacred
Heart Academy*

*Pages 32-33:
Original SHA
building, 1877*

*Six year old Rosa Lee Amshoff,
youngest boarder at Sacred
Heart Academy*

*Opposite page: Graduates
1910, 2002*

of the campus, again on land purchased for expansion. Over the next four decades, major renovations to the "new" Sacred Heart included additions of a state-of-the-art technology and fine arts wing, a new 750-capacity gym, athletic fields for soccer, field hockey and softball, a new track, new five-court tennis complex and two field houses.

And so, the seeds of Ursuline education, so full of promise when they first flowered in Louisville's German-immigrant neighborhoods of the 19th century, spread to the city's vibrant, blossoming suburban edge—where they took root and flourished. Despite the many changes of location and differing styles of architecture, despite the addition of acreage and the expansion of uses for her "country" landscape, Sacred Heart Academy remained throughout the 20th century the heartwood of the Lexington Road campus.

Today, as yesterday, the Academy is the campus anchor. As these pages illustrate, Sacred Heart Academy is and always has been the core of the campus. As it enters its 126th year, it remains a thriving academy, supplying an excellent education and a nurturing environment to young women of the 21st century.

Sacred Heart Academy
students on campus, 1909

SHA students, 1917

Academy of the Sacred Heart

3115 CHEROKEE DRIVE

LOUISVILLE, KENTUCKY

June 15, 1918

1. F. Kernan for her daughter Margaret.

To Ursuline Sisters, Dr.

Matriculation Fee,	$	5.00	
Board and Tuition,		167.20	
Music Lessons,		50.00	
Books and Library,		7.00	
Sheet Music and Studies,		3.50	
Needle Work Material,		1.00	
~~Art Lessons,~~ *Uniform Hat*		1.50	
Art Material,			
Elocution Lessons,			
Sundries: Med. Lect. and Gym. Fees,		6.50	
~~Laboratory Fee,~~ *Luncheon (May & June)*		7.00	
Graduation Fee,			
Graduation Expense,			
rent $225.00 (M. Ruhm)		$243.70	
		$223.00	
	Balance	20.70	

*"Every Wednesday morning
in 1917, we took long, brisk
walks with faculty members.
When we took walks with Father,
you could see all the way to
St. Matthews. There was a white
house where Holy Spirit church
is now, but that was the only
house I can remember seeing
along the way."*

—Otillia (Sr. Mary George) Hubbuch '17

*Sacred Heart Academy,
1903-1918*

Above: Sacred Heart Academy's chapel before the fire of 1918

Opposite page top: Photo of fire from The Courier-Journal

Lower right: Charred altar stone found in the rubble after the fire

THE GREAT FIRE, 1918

The afternoon of Friday, April 19, 1918 was anything but typical at SHA. Students diligently studying under the guidance of the Ursuline Sisters were horrified to smell smoke and see flames skirting through their school. Sister Mary Ruth Clemens quickly escorted her French class to safety, then returned to the building to ring the five call bells continuously, alerting the other sisters and students of the fire. Its origin was never officially determined.

When she finally escaped the smoke and flames, Sister Mary Ruth recalled seeing the entire roof ablaze. "We stood at a distance and saw our beloved school burn to the ground in about three hours. Steel beams bent like hair pins in the intense heat. The bell tower and bell were never found. We took it for granted that the bell melted away. As the flames licked their way through the building, we shed tears for our favorite rooms, the library, the chapel, classrooms, dormitories, and we just knew what prized possessions were turned into ashes."

The Courier-Journal reported "...most of the girls suffered smarting eyes, but none were in danger except Beulah Minney, who was left in a class room when the rest of the children marched out." Two of Beulah's classmates noticed she was missing and ran back in the burning building to rescue their friend, who suffered from smoke inhalation.

The Courier Journal told of "...hundreds who flocked to the scene on foot, in automobiles and other conveyances. Automobiles stretched for a long distance along the highways leading to the academy, where they had been abandoned by automobilists

who gave aid. A high wind continued throughout the fire. Perhaps the most spectacular scenes were witnessed when walls began falling while the flames were at their height. As a wall crashed, there rose above the dense smoke and sharp flames thick clouds of dust. Mother Angela, with the other nuns, lined up the pupils and watched the flames, weeping silently as the walls went down."

Hot spots erupted overnight, burning the wall between SHA and the original mansion. Firefighters saved the mansion, but SHA lay in ashes.

Over the next week and a half, the Ursuline Sisters, led by Sister Mary Joseph Dunn, mobilized to clean, paint, and gather new furniture. Several enterprising sisters simultaneously embarked on an ambitious city-wide fundraising effort. Ten days later, SHA reopened for business in temporary quarters in the recently built motherhouse and in the Model School.

—*Laura Guetig '86*

Above: Graduates, 1922

Below: Blessing at the site of the new Sacred Heart Academy building, 1924

Sacred Heart Academy, Louisville, Ky.
A Resident and Day School for Girls and Young Women

THE High School offers the standard course of four years to complete the program of secondary education and to qualify its graduates for admittance into college. This School is affiliated with the Catholic University of America, Washington, D. C., and is formally accredited by the University of Kentucky and the Association of Colleges and Secondary Schools of the Southern States.

SCHOOL OF MUSIC, FINE ARTS AND EXPRESSION

CONDUCTED BY THE URSULINE SISTERS

ADDRESS: THE PRINCIPAL, SACRED HEART ACADEMY
3107 LEXINGTON ROAD   LOUISVILLE, KENTUCKY

Sacred Heart Academy, 1926

SHA students, 1927

"My mother and sisters remembered watching the flames from Hillcrest Avenue in 1918, so it was exciting to be one of the first students in the newly constructed school. The sisters always took a personal interest in the girls, wanting them to be bright young women. Even today, at 92 years old, I still say with pride, I went to Sacred Heart Academy."

—Eleanor (Sister Martha Maria, SCN)
   Guetig '29

Sacred Heart students, 1931

Above: Seniors, 1933

Opposite page: Class of 1934

Students in hats, 1934

*"As if but yesterday we recall...
we became most patriotic this
year...for the first time our
Minute Man flag waved
proudly beneath "Old Glory."
The flag was a symbol of
honor bestowed by the United
States Government for the
students being one hundred
percent and the leading school
in Louisville in purchasing
war bonds and stamps."*

—1942 Angeline

Students, 1945

Winter, 1950

Aerial of Ursuline Campus, 1954

That <u>noise</u> you hear is <u>progress</u>! This new Sacred Heart Academy Building is a part of the Greater Ursuline Expansion Program

Above: Sacred Heart Academy, 1964

Opposite page: Groundbreaking for new SHA building, 1962

*Left: Prayer service for
POWs and MIAs, 1972*

*Opposite page: SHA
parking lot, 1968*

*"SHA helped me understand
the role a high quality
educational program would
play in my life and offered
a great platform for the critical
thinking that college would
demand and life would expect.
I am close to many of my
classmates today and
exprience a bond of friendship
that remains perhaps the most
special reward SHA has*

to offer."

—Maria Imorde Gerwing Hampton '65
   Executive Director,
   The Housing Partnership
   of Louisville

Groundbreaking for a $10 million
total campus renovation, 1998

Above: Construction of new gym, 1999

*Opposite page top: New field house
and track under construction, 1999*

*Opposite page bottom: Newly
finished tennis courts, 1999*

Sacred Heart Academy gym, 2000

Above and opposite page:
Art, Media and Technology
Wing, 2001

"I can still see the visions of hockey games, the Brown Jug, plays, proms, school assemblies, retreats, club meetings, Sr. Vivian's English classes, Miss Herp's biology class, our white graduation gowns...and the red roses. I have been privileged to be one of the many graduates of SHA in its first 125 years. May those young women who carry on the tradition continue to keep the memories of our school in their hearts forever."

—Dr. Dorothy Eilers Mitchell-Leef '67
Endocrinologist

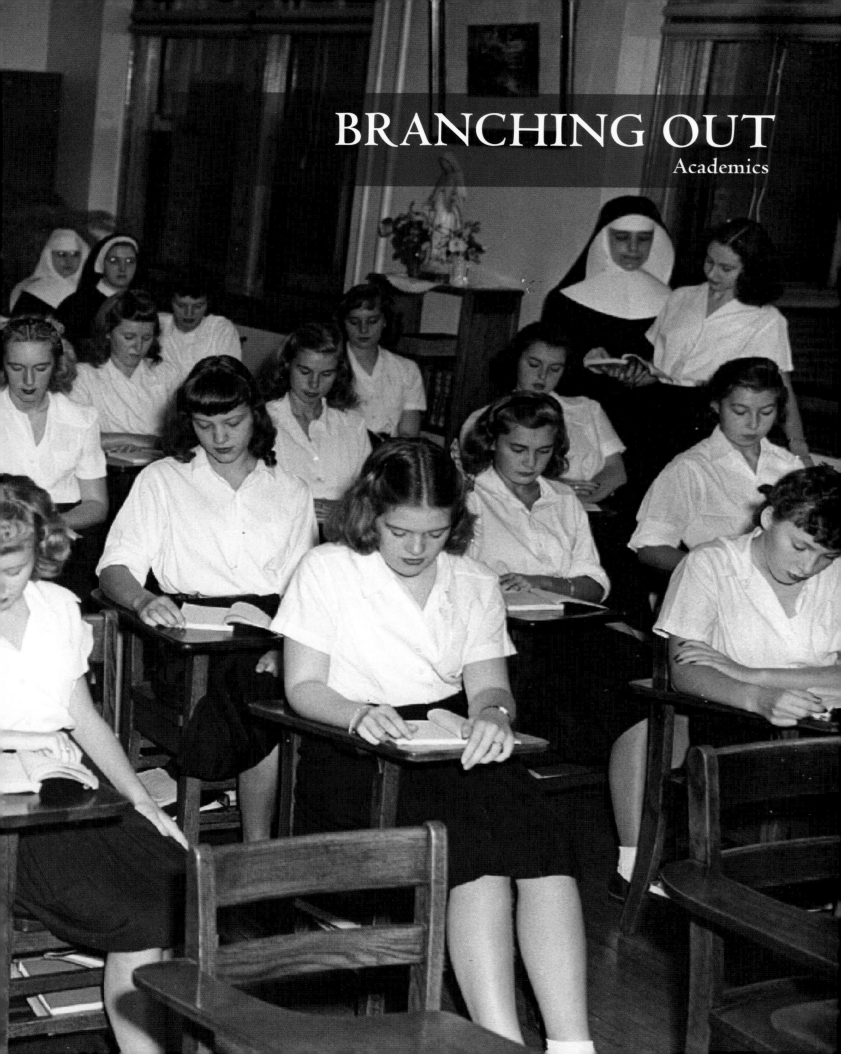

BRANCHING OUT
Academics

BRANCHING OUT

Academics

Courage and joy and a shining start

From the October day in 1877 when Sacred Heart Academy opened its doors, its mission has been clear: to prepare students to meet the needs of a changing world. Sacred Heart students, at the outset, were encouraged to explore a variety of subjects, to branch out academically, to learn to find balance among many interests.

Education, particularly the education of young women, had long been an Ursuline ideal. The sisters traced it back to the early 16th century, to the life of their founder, Saint Angela Merici. She, too, was committed to serving the needs of her day. So it was no surprise that the Louisville Ursulines, who already had succeeded in establishing one girls' academy, would set their academic sights high when they opened Sacred Heart Academy in 1877.

From the start, the school encouraged its students to challenge themselves academically. As early as 1883, Sacred Heart students wrote and produced a play at a downtown opera house in honor of the Ursulines' 25th anniversary in Louisville. According to a school manual from the 1930s, students were expected to strive for "a harmonious development of the whole personality."

The sisters hoped to "develop and discipline the mind, the heart, and the will of the sincere American Girl in order that she may be prepared to meet with fearlessness and faith the unique difficulties of this age in which she lives."

Sacred Heart Academy's first commencement was held in 1888, two years before the Battle of Wounded Knee, and a decade before the Spanish American War was waged. In 1919 the Academy, by then a fully accredited Kentucky school, became an affiliated school of the Catholic University of America. From day one, the curriculum included academic subjects as well as courses in the arts and business, including, at various times, landscape sketching, music, elocution and typing.

The tradition continues. Ninety-two percent of Sacred Heart's faculty today have masters degrees or beyond. And in recent years, 99 percent of its grads have gone on to higher education. From Sacred Heart, which was named a national Blue Ribbon School of Excellence by the U.S. Department of Education in 1998 and is the only Catholic school in Kentucky to be accepted into the International Baccalaureate program, these young women have branched out to more than 100 different schools in 31 states and the District of Columbia.

Sacred Heart's illustrious alumnae represent many professional fields, from biomedical research to business to the arts. Today they lead corporations, write books, serve their communities as doctors and lawyers and elected officials, and uphold the Ursuline commitment to education as teachers and mentors.

—Dianne Aprile '67

Science lab, 1926

Pages 86-87: Sister Francelle Otte's class, 1940s

Sacred Heart Academy library, 1908

"Sacred Heart Academy is the embodiment of an ideal. Its very atmosphere breathes the influence to develop and discipline the mind, the heart, and the will of the sincere American Girl in order that she may be prepared to meet with fearlessness and faith the unique difficulties of this age in which she lives."

—Sacred Heart Academy brochure, 1933

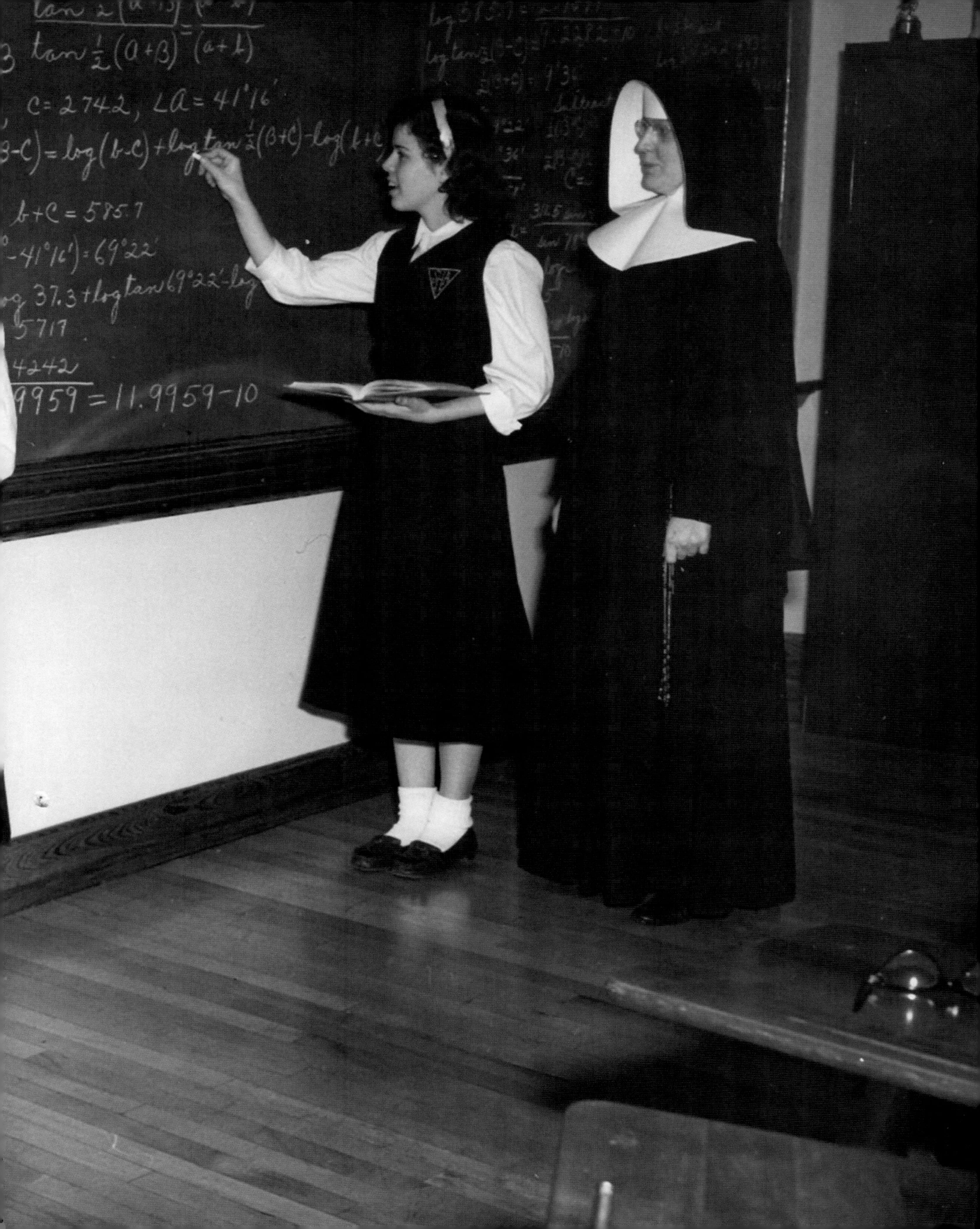
c = 274.2, ∠a = 41°16'
b+c = 585.7
9959 = 11.9959-10

"My philosophy of teaching originates from my own learning experiences. Learning must permeate all facets of a person's life or it has no real value. The greatest thing to me is to see someone's eyes light up and say 'I understand.'"

—Mary Jane Herp
Science, French teacher
1947-1989

Physics at Kentucky Kingdom

"Sacred Heart made it easy to explore and develop into what you wanted to be, and you were always encouraged by the faculty and staff to follow your dreams and be the best you can be."

—Anne Sutherland Reuter '89
Cryogenic Cooling Researcher

National Honor Society induction, 1997

SACRED HEART ACADEMY

STUDENT GRADE REPORT

COURSE DESCRIPTION	COURSE NO.	FIRST SEMESTER								SECOND SEMESTER								FINAL GRADE	CREDIT
		1ST QTR.		2ND QTR.		EXAM.	AVG.	3RD QTR.		4TH QTR.		EXAM.	AVG.					
		GRADE	CONDUCT	GRADE	CONDUCT			GRADE	CONDUCT	GRADE	CONDUCT							
FAMILY LIVING	0414A	97	S	98	S		98										98	.50
MORALITY	0424B							95	S	98	S		97				97	.50
ENGLISH IV	1460	93	S	96	S	98	95	96	S	94	S	92	92				94	1.00
JOURNALISM	1493A	98	S	99	S		99										99	.50
PRE-CAL/CAL	2030	94	S	94	S	84	92	93	S	99	S	96	96				94	1.00
TRIGONOMETRY	2741A	97	S	93	S	91	94										94	.50
COMPUTER PROG	2841B							93	S	92	S	85	91				91	.50
US GOVERNMENT	3551	94	S	94	S		94	97	S	97	S		97				96	1.00
BUS PRINCIPLES	7821B							98	S	99	S		99				99	.50

SCHOOL YEAR	85-86	DAYS ABSENT ▶	0	0	GPA 3.750	0	0	TOTAL ABSENT ▶	0
		TIMES TARDY ▶	0	0		0	0	TOTAL TARDY ▶	0

	HOME ROOM 103	RANK IN CLASS CUR 1/217 ACC 4/217	STUDENT NAME
STUDENT NO.	HOME ROOM	RANK IN CLASS	STUDENT NAME

STUDENT COPY

Certificate of  Membership

National Honor Society
of
Secondary Schools

This Certifies that

JEANNIE LECHLEITER

was elected a member

of the   COR JESU   Chapter

of the

National Honor Society of Secondary Schools,

membership in which is based on

Scholarship, Leadership, Service, and Character.

Given at   Sacred Heart Academy

this   7th   day of   May   19 86

Scott D. Thomson
SECRETARY

ADVISER *Mary Ann Desing*

Terrence J. Giroux
DIRECTOR,
OFFICE OF STUDENT ACTIVITIES

Sister Louise Marie Willenbrink
PRINCIPAL

Above and opposite page:
Sacred Heart Academy named
national Blue Ribbon School
of Excellence, 1998

"To me, it is a sense of giving people hope that things can be different and that someone believes in them."

—Carol Zurkuhlen King '62

In 1999, shortly before Carol lost her battle with cancer, she and her husband Nick established the King Scholar Program, which currently provides scholarships for 19 academically motivated Sacred Heart Academy students of diverse racial and socio-economic backgrounds.

SHA is the only Catholic high school and one of three schools in Kentucky which offer the International Baccalaureate Program. IB students receive specialized diplomas and advanced credit at many colleges and universities worldwide.

"I'll always be grateful I went to Sacred Heart...
for the spiritual grounding, the educational
discipline, the athletic challenges, the journey of
understanding social issues, for the fun and the
safe environment...but most of all for the
mentors and friends she gave me for my lifetime."

—Elaine "Cissy" Musselman '61
Insurance Executive

"SHA is special because it is a place dedicated to the liberal arts, it attracts bright and committed students, and the teachers care and have personal relationships with their students. For me, the Ursuline Sisters were the first true 'women's libbers' I knew!"

—Joan Riehm '63
Public Issues
Communications Consultant

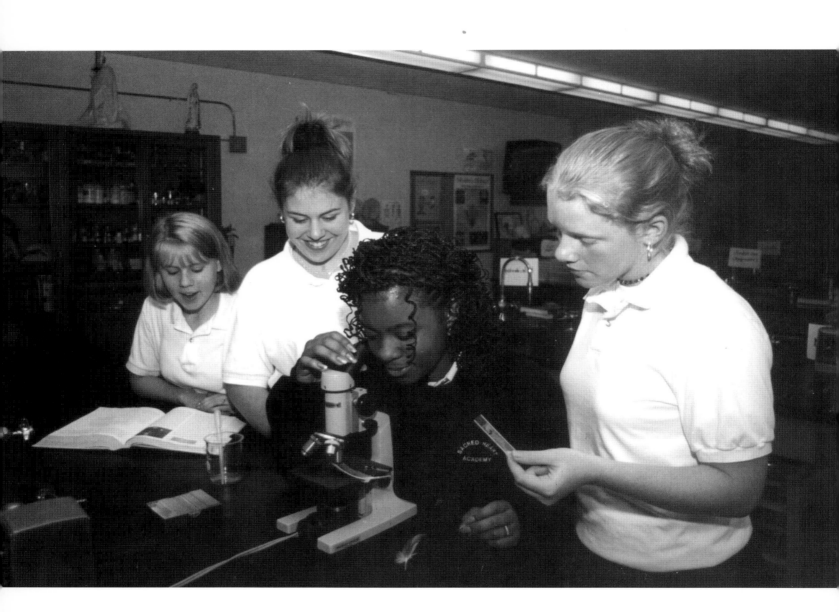

STRONG LIMBS
Athletics

STRONG LIMBS
Athletics

Daring to try, hearts beating high

The ideal of a balanced life was, from the start, an important element of the philosophy of Sacred Heart Academy. Its founders believed in helping students become well-rounded individuals, neither too bookish nor too playful.

Sports were always deemed an important part of the educational process. Witness a 1933 recruiting brochure, which noted: "Since mental labor exhausts and dulls the sensibilities, provision is made for such sports and activities as are conducive to healthful living and the acquisition of the coordinated rhythmical movements so necessary to general well-being."

Almost from the beginning, students at Sacred Heart could participate in a variety of athletic activities. Horseback riding was an early favorite, enjoyed at nearby Cherokee and Seneca Parks. By 1926, when the "new" school replaced the one that burned, SHA sported a volleyball club, cheerleaders and a tennis club. However, all teams were originally

intramural, since the sisters felt that to compete with other schools would "diminish the love of the game."

Some things do change. Sacred Heart has long been producing competitors of the first order, not only on a local level but against world-class athletes as well. Today, the school's record includes the capture of more than 60 state championships, more than any other girls' program in Kentucky, and it can boast a graduate who is an Olympic gold medalist.

Just as important as those stunning statistics, however, are the irreplaceable life lessons learned through playing sports, a by-product of athletics that the early leaders of Sacred Heart most certainly had in mind.

Alumnae from all walks of life refer to the role that team sports played for them in terms of learning to work with other people under pressure and problem-solving as a group, whether it's at home, at the office or at a town meeting.

—Dianne Aprile '67

Basketball team, 1934

Pages 114-115: Hockey, 1940s

Tennis Club, 1927

Horseback riding, Seneca Park, 1931

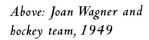

Above: Joan Wagner and hockey team, 1949

Right: The Little Brown Jug

Opposite page: Sally Parsons Roby Kampschaefer with hockey team, 1960s

Bunny Daugherty and hockey team

"From 1973 to 1998, Bunny Daugherty coached 209 seasons—40 of basketball, 37 of both field hockey and volleyball, 25 each of golf, track and tennis, and 10 of gymnastics and swimming — most of it at SHA. She taught all the girls she coached that 'if you knock the 't' off of can't, you can.' I've never forgotten that, and I'll never forget Bunny Daugherty and the impact she has had on my life and on so many others."

—Donna Bender Moir '79
SHA Athletic Director

Above: Field hockey team, 1967

Right: "Mother" Betty Volz, varsity field hockey coach, holding "The Mug"

Opposite page: State field hockey champs, 2001

©*photo courtesy of* The Courier-Journal

*Above: Sally Parsons Roby
Kampschaefer and swim team, 1960s*

*Opposite page top: State record
set by relay team*

*Opposite page bottom: Swim
team, 1999*

Above: Leigh Ann Fetter Witt '89, first woman in the world to break the 22 second barrier in the 50-yard freestyle

Left: Caroline Burkle '04, broke Kentucky's oldest record in the 500-yard freestyle, set in 1983 by Kara McGrath, also from SHA

©*photo courtesy of* The Courier-Journal

Opposite page: Mary T. Meagher Plant '83 ("Madame Butterfly"), three-time Olympic competitor, winner of three gold medals for swimming in the 1984 Olympics

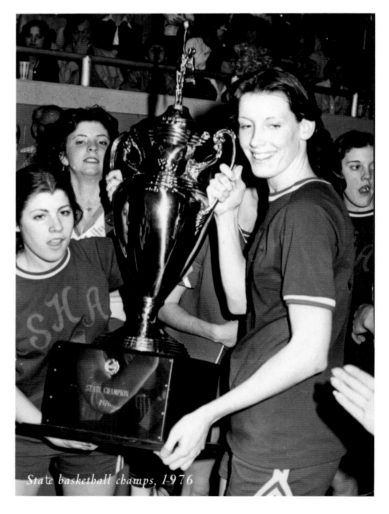

State basketball champs, 1976

State basketball champs, 2002
led by coach Donna Bender Moir '79

Above: Carly Ormerod '05, the only freshman ever named MVP in a state basketball championship

Opposite page: Crystal Kelly '04, ranked as one of the Top Ten sophomore players in the nation.

MILESTONES IN SACRED HEART ACADEMY SPORTS: 1877-2002

1926
Intramural volleyball, tennis and cheerleading are established.

1930
SHA's first competitive field hockey team, dressed in sailor-tops and navy bloomers, takes on Kentucky Home School for their first game. During this inaugural SHA sports event, one SHA player accidentally knocks the teeth out of a Kentucky Home School player with a bad swing of the hockey stick.

1937
The Catholic Girls' Basketball League is formed, but due to the disastrous 1937 flood, no games are played all season.

1937
SHA establishes a horseback riding club based at Rock Creek Riding Stables.

1940
The SHA field hockey team wins its first of many titles: League Champs.

1944
JV field hockey and JV basketball begin, with coaches Irma Schalk and Mary Gratzer Bush '38.

1945
One hundred students march to Seneca Park singing the SHA fight song as a show of support for a struggling team—hence the birth of the 100 Club.

1948
Miss Mary Jane Herp becomes SHA's bowling coach.

1945-54
Coach Joan Wagner Hammer '45 leads the varsity field hockey and basketball teams to many victories and league championships.

1961
The Academy League in tennis is founded under coach Sally Parsons Roby Kampschaefer '51.

1962
The first of 19 state championships is won by the SHA swim team.

1963
SHA's first track team takes the field.

1964
SHA's bowling team takes home 28 trophies in the city tourney.

1969
SHA loses the state championship in swimming by two points, but the team, Coach Sally Parsons Roby Kampschaefer '51 and several supporters in the stands take a plunge in the pool after the competition.

1971
SHA's bowling team goes co-ed with Trinity High School.

1973
Bunny Daugherty is named SHA Athletic Director.

1974
Mary Stivers '75, Carla Amlung '76, Missy Brown '78, Tina Keller Poulsen '76, Jessie Bollinger '76 and Nell Pearce Bradley '75 are named to the All State Basketball Team.

1976
The fencing team is formed and is state runner-up.

1978
First year for cross country

1979
State runners-up in gymnastics

1981
First year for varsity softball

1984
Mary T. Meagher '83 ("Madame Butterfly") wins three gold medals for swimming in the 1984 Olympics.

1986
SHA's varsity basketball team wins the LIT, led by all time leading SHA scorer Susan Yates Ely '86 (2,071 career points) and second all time SHA scorer Dawn Brohman '86 (1,644 career points).

1991
Donna Bender Moir '79 is named Athletic Director.

Varsity soccer comes to SHA.

1993
Kelly Brown Grimes '86 is named Volleyball Coach of the Year.

1995
SHA cross country is ranked in top 30 in the United States.

1997
SHA's cheerleading team is National COA Runner-up.

1999
SHA's first rowing team, named Midwest Region Champs.

2001
Field Hockey State Champs

SHA's varsity cheerleading team shows the nation's brightest school spirit as it wins the national American Spirit Championship.

2002
SHA's basketball team wins the LIT for the second consecutive year, and wins the state championship.

Donna Bender Moir '79 is named Kentucky Basketball Coach of the Year.

Above: Cheerleaders, 1944

Left: Cheerleaders, 1963

Opposite page top: Dance team

Opposte page bottom: JV cheerleaders win national championship, 2002

SHA STATE CHAMPIONSHIPS

Basketball	Gymnastics
1978	1977
1995	1978
2002	

Cross Country	Swimming
1994	1963
	1964
	1978
Fencing	1979
1970	1980
1972	1981
1978	1982
	1983
Field Hockey	1984
1983	1985
1986	1986
2001	1987
	1988
Golf	1995
1984	1996
1985	1997
1986	1998
1987	1999
1993	2000

Tennis	Singles	Doubles
1987	1964	1967
1988	1965	1974
1989	1968	1975
1990	1969	1977
1991	1970	1981
	1971	1987
	1972	1988
	1973	1989
	1974	1990
	1990	1991
	1991	1999

Betsy Jones, 1965

"We're loyal to you, SHA
Your white and your blue, SHA
We'll back you to stand,
You're the best in the land,
For your colors are true, SHA.
Rah! Rah! Rah!
Bring out your blue and your white,
Bring out your colors so bright.
We'll show you our loyalty
By our victory for dear old SHA."

—SHA pep song

VALKYRIE
HALL OF FAME

1990
Sally Parsons Kampschaefer '51
Lois Langan '58
Donna Grimes '73
Mary Jane Hoben '72
Missy Brown '78
Donna Bender Moir '79

1991
Betty Zollinger Volz '49
Kay Corcoran Whelan '62
Ginger Eckert Howe '64
Karen Gocke '65
Cissy Maloney '72
Judy McDonald Burkman '77
Beth Stegner Peabody '79
Joan Wagner Hammer '45
Mary Gratzer Bush '38

1992
Sr. Louise Marie Willenbrink '52
Elaine "Cissy" Musselman '61
Teri Tafel Wells '72
Carla Amlung '76
Jessie Bollinger '76
Tina Keller Poulsen '76
Robin Brown Schmidt '79
Susan Elpers Inman '81
Mary T. Meagher Plant '83
Bunny Daugherty

1993
Anne Zollinger Schlegel '41
Jane Walker Rowan '52
Mary Ann Bender Vogt '56
Alice Driscoll Buchart '63
Jamie Wadell '71
Mary Stivers '75
Barbara Elpers Sheran '78
Liz Sadtler Lewis '80

1994
Suzanne Whelan Timperman '57
Kathy Beckman '62
Pam Higgs Martin '75
Sally Carpenter Boven '76
Nina Leigh Howard '79
Emily Wolfe Grady '80

1995
Pat Stauble Bailey '49
Barbara Heck Vonderheide '51
Chris Sheridan Curl '75
Jeannie Kleinert Rueff '75
Tami Conti '83
Pete Peterson

1996
Jane Miranda Elpers '55
Pat Lally Minton '65
Barbara Erickson '71
Alicia Oberst '84
Dawn Brohman '86
Susan Yates Ely '86

1997
Joyce Andriot Watson '61
Carol Kunk Butler '68
Rose Elpers Weterer '77
Missy Gahm Kremer '87

1998
Colleen Jones Underhill '74
Susan Mercke Stewart '78
Julie Gering Zaber '87

1999
Leigh Ann Fetter Witt '87
Kelly Brown Grimes '86
Pamela Willinger Stallings '82

2000
Mary Carmel Mudd Borders '67
Marion Veeneman Panyon '60

2001
Kathy Lally '66
Diane Strothman Keefe '89

2002
Vinnie Wise Brotzge '75
Kimberly Jedlicki Buchheid '83
Judith Condon Dostal '64

Elpers family with four Hall of Famers

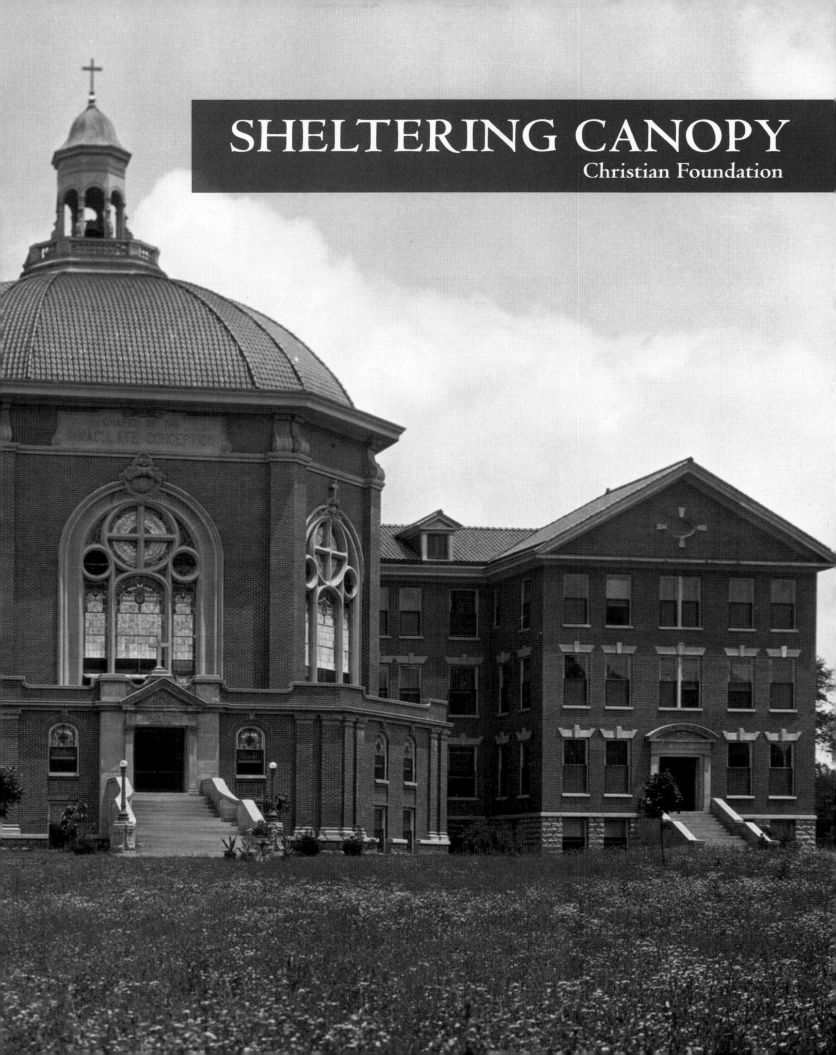

SHELTERING CANOPY
Christian Foundation

SHELTERING CANOPY
Christian Foundation

Lovely the virtues that set you apart

Unselfish service to one's community—both the spiritual side of it and the civic side—is a cornerstone of Sacred Heart Academy's philosophy. The Ursulines, building on Saint Angela's devotion to attending the needs of others, wove this idea of service into the very fabric of the school's identity.

Through the decades, the sisters' dedication to doing God's work through serving others spilled over to their students. This aspect of Angeline spirituality was passed on not only in religion classes but through the give-and-take between teacher and student. Its by-products have been many. Traditionally, until the 1960s, a few seniors each year would announce their calling to become an Ursuline Sister. Generations of Sacred Heart alums cherish memories of graduation Masses in the chapel and unforgettable conversations at senior retreats; they remember those events as vividly as they recall hockey games at Seneca Park and what they wore to the Senior Prom.

Today, Sacred Heart students still build upon the strong ethical foundation laid down by the sisters who founded their school. Their decisions to perform volunteer work in Appalachia during spring break or their commitment to social justice in Central America reflect their school's enduring values.

These values are also evident in the lives of graduates who are devoting their careers to building a better world.

For its hometown, Sacred Heart Academy has produced many civic leaders, including a member of Congress, the first female chairperson of the Board of Aldermen, a Deputy Mayor, judges and others.

Many of these service-minded alums are recipients of the Heart Award, established in 1991, to honor "a graduate who has contributed in a significant way to her community and/or to the lives of those around her."

For many graduates, early inspiration for their later lives came during annual retreats. As early as 1908, this tradition was already well-established. SHA retreats changed with the times, sometimes being held on campus and sometimes off, evolving from silent, contemplative retreats to ones that emphasized scripture study or group dynamics. Then as now, the goal of the retreat was to encourage students' deeper reflection upon and greater connection to their spiritual selves.

Like a shade tree that provides comfort to those in need of rest and safety, Sacred Heart has served as a sheltering canopy of ethical, spiritual and civic responsibility throughout its history—from the 1937 flood, when it opened its arms to Ohio River refugees, to the horror of September 11, 2001, when students, in the wake of terrorists' attacks on the United States, mobilized a blood drive, organized a prayer service and collected donations for victims.

—Dianne Aprile '67

May Procession, 1941

Pages 154-155:
Motherhouse chapel, 1921

Above: Freshman Religion class, 2001

Opposite page top: Retreat, 1967

Opposite page bottom: Retreat

*Sacred Heart Academy students
volunteering in Appalachia*

"*The most special memories
I have of SHA are the
wonderful friends I had who
shared so many of the same
values, goals and dreams and
the teachers who gave themselves
so selflessly that we might
become high achievers both
academically and personally.*"

—Anne Meagher Northup '66
Member of Congress,
Third District, Kentucky

"SHA taught me to believe in myself and to go after my dreams. I can't help stop hunger by dreaming that somebody is feeding hungry kids. I need to go out there and find the best way to teach others. A team approach is the best approach. I definitely learned that playing sports at SHA. You have a common goal, and as a team, you go for it!"

—Nancy Russman '68
  Executive Director Kids Café and
  Executive Chef for Louisville's
  Dare to Care Food Bank

Sacred Heart Academy students
volunteering in Appalachia, 1997

Opposite page bottom: Student
visiting the residents of
Marian Home

"*SHA prepared me well for college and beyond, and instilled in me the value and importance of Catholic schools.*"

—Barbara Lechleiter McGrath '72
Co-founder of a South Carolina
Catholic high school modeled in
part on her SHA education.

HEART AWARD RECIPIENTS

1991
Susan King Jones '73
Mary Jane Herp
Mary Alice Maloney McIntyre '45
Norma Oberst
Colleen Wickham Sparks '57

1992
Cynthia Rouseve Highfield
Mary Julia Eifler Kuhn '66
Floy Terstegge Meagher
Steven Schoo
Marilyn Schuler '50
Judith Brady Wayne
Thomas Weis
Shelley Fitzpatrick Wohlleb '67

1993
Mary Jo Hand Weller '68
Robert Lockhart
G. Raymond Schuhmann
Sr. George Marie Long
Carol Zurkuhlen King '62
Jean Willenbrink Perrone '50

1994
Judy Schroeder Watrous '68
Barbara Pierce MacDonald '59
Mary Lee Reilly Boyett
Carol Kunk Butler '68
Ann Ecker Dreisbach '67

1995
Jeanne Huber Ferguson '63
Susan Bauer '68
Cynthia Collins Shain '69

1996
Barbara Siebert Aubrey '62
Mary Ann Zumer
Richardson '52
Myrian Bodner
John Kraus

1997
Valerie Bertoli Pogue '68
Martha Brotzge Weinert '67

1998
Betty Meyer Carney '61
Michael Hendricks

1999
Patricia Smith Daley '50
Anne Palmer Dueitt
Elizabeth Corcoran Vish '70

2000
Ruth Dilger Kelly '66
Joyce Keibler
Robert Tonini

2001
Lane Goulet
Laura Guetig '86
Anne Thomas

2002
Barbara Duerr Trompeter '50
Carolyn Reed '77
Noreen Fenton
Angie Gimmel

Alumnae Board, 1908

ALUMNA OF THE YEAR
1981-2002

Nancy Schneider O'Hearn '63

Elaine "Cissy" Musselman '61

Ellen Boone Greenwell Camentz '60

Sr. Louise Marie Willenbrink '52

Sr. Marlene Oetken '50

Mary Pat Nolan '68

Louisa "Weda" Riehm '58

Barbara Golden Cambron '63

Joan Riehm '63

Melissa Mershon '71

Helen Mohlenkamp Ulmer '51

Maria Imorde Gerwing Hampton '65

Dianne Aprile '67

Anne Meagher Northup '66

Sharon Virginia Hurley '49

Terese Kearns Pfister '70

Nancy Russman '68

Barbara Siebert Aubrey '62

Mary Louise Willenbrink Schrodt '47

Marion Veeneman Panyan '60

Sr. Paula Kleine-Kracht '64

Karen Gruneisen '76

Alumnae Board, 2002

The tragic events of September 11, 2001 affected everyone. SHA students, moved by the enormity of the tragedy, launched into action with prayers and student-organized blood drives. At students' urging, silence was observed in the hallways during class changes and more than $1,000 was raised in Red Cross donations. On September 14, the National Day of Mourning, SHA and other Ursuline Campus students, along with Ursuline Sisters, faculty, staff and neighbors drew strength from each other's hearts with a 1,000 person-strong prayer service on campus. Beneath a blue sky and the American flag, flying somberly at half-mast, the Ursuline Campus gathered in prayer and song.

TENDING NEW SHOOTS
Faculty

TENDING NEW SHOOTS
Faculty

We shall remember and love you, we vow

The first faculty of Sacred Heart were Ursuline Sisters, women trained in Saint Angela's ideals. Their motto reflected their dedication to education, and their actions testified to the strength of that dedication. The faculty were, after all, sorely tested in the school's early years.

Barely two decades after opening the school in 1877, they were already about the task of raising money to build a "new" Sacred Heart. Then, not many years after proudly opening that architect-designed school building, the sisters watched it go up in flames. The moving and fundraising started all over again.

But the spirit of Sacred Heart Academy was always to meet whatever challenges came its way. And so the sisters erected one "new" building after another to accommodate growing enrollments and changing times. In adversity, teachers and students developed a spirit of team work and common purpose.

Even in the earliest yearbooks, there is evidence of strong bonds of friendship between students and faculty. Teachers are remembered with awe and affection. Mention is made of the bittersweetness of Graduation Day, when ties between mentor and pupil were

loosened. There is also evidence of many happy reunions, both planned and impromptu, that prove Sacred Heart ties may be loosened but never undone.

Alumnae also fondly recall certain priests who taught and preached retreats at the academy. One of them, Father Daniel Lord, the Jesuit from St. Louis who wrote Sacred Heart's school song, was a frequent guest, remembered as a moving public speaker and a fine pianist who often played informally for students.

The Ursulines who taught—and still teach—at Sacred Heart include many faculty legends. The very mention of their names evokes vivid memories: unique voices and distinguishing movements, pet phrases and gleaming smiles of approval (yes, withering glares of disapproval, too.) Some of them, like the long-lived Sister Antonia Wagner, were an influence on generations of Sacred Heart graduates. Others, like Sister Brendan Conlon (who, after leaving the faculty, went to work with the poor and powerless of Appalachia) continue to inspire students and alums to follow their lead and help heal our broken world.

—Dianne Aprile '67

The Faculty

Sr Marie
My music teacher

Sr Ruth
Freshman +
sophomore
teacher.

Memory book, 1921

Sister Mary Joseph
my favorite. She
was principal of S. W. A.
when I started. My
music teacher for
three years after
the building burnt
she was so nervous
that Mother Angela
sent her to Nebraska.
It nearly broke my
heart to see her leave
She is now directress of
St Patrick Academy in
Sidney Nebraska.

The Faculty

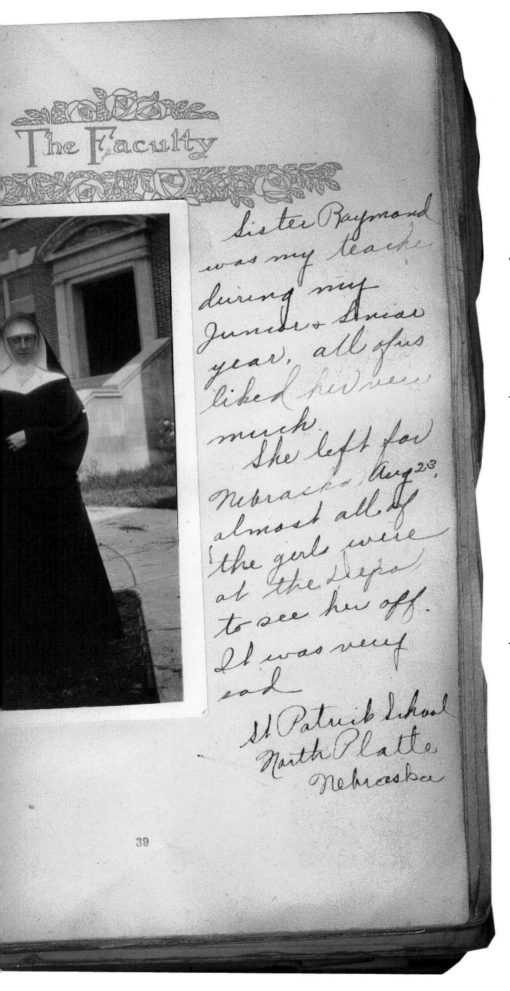

Sister Raymond was my teacher during my Junior & Senior year, all of us liked her very much.

She left for Nebraska, Aug 23, almost all of the girls were at the Depot to see her off. It was very sad.

St Patrick School
North Platte
Nebraska

"My memories of Sacred Heart include the outstanding Sister Thomasita, who convinced me to stick with math, my eventual teaching field. SHA is unique because it exemplifies what is outstanding in Ursuline education—development of the whole person, recognizing the talents and gifts of each individual, challenging young women to stretch beyond what they think they can do, and doing all of this without regard for where they live or how much money their parents earn."

—Sister Paula Kleine-Kracht '64
Principal, SHA 1994-2001
Teacher, SHA 1969-1972

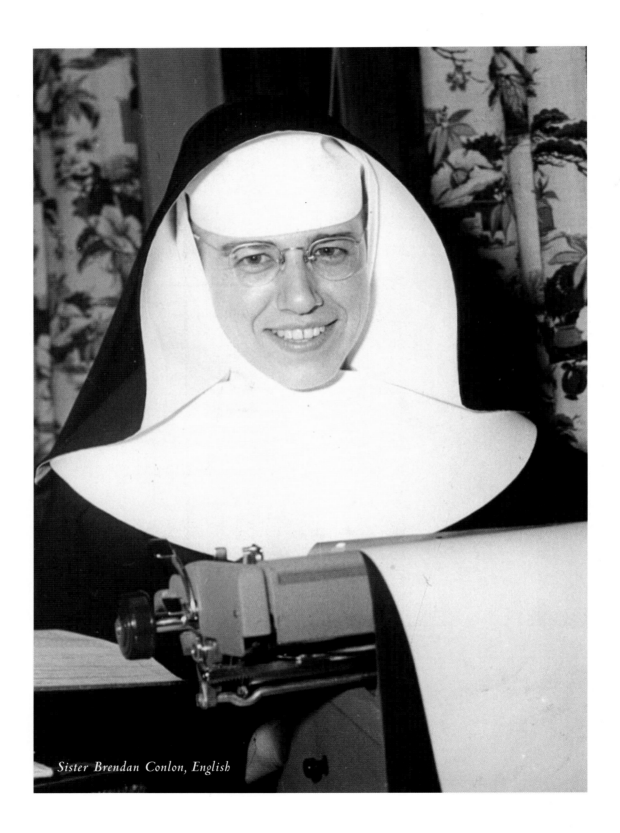

Sister Brendan Conlon, English

Sister Antonia Wagner '19, Latin

"Sister Antonia, lover of Latin, still glides into my thoughts now and then, most often when I'm ready to give up on a challenge, when I need to be reminded of the poetry in perseverance. She stands there, her beloved 'Aeneid' in hand, smiling patiently at me as I enumerate the many reasons why I can't do whatever it is I'm afraid to try. Her smile's what I can't resist. It's so encouraging, so full of the faith in me that I lack. I struggle on, though, and soon she's got me back in the rhythm of things, remembering the basics, the rules you can always fall back on. Amo, Amas, Amat. Sometimes it's as simple as that."

—Dianne Aprile '67
From *The Things We Don't Forget:
Views From Real Life.*

Mary Jane Herp, Biology
and French, Bowling Coach

"Whether it's to ask about college transcripts, to talk about next year's schedule, to discuss that low math grade, or just to chat about teenage interests, every SHAer knows that Sr. George Marie will take time out for a talk. We'll always remember her encouraging us to intellectual and spiritual striving and holding up to us high and beautiful ideals of Christian womanhood."

—*The Angeline*

Sister George Marie Long
Principal, 1958-1968

Sister Vivian Dreisbach, English

Sister Colette Kraemer '50, English

SACRED HEART ACADEMY PRINCIPALS

1877	Sister Mary Florence Meder
1892	Sister M. Augusta Bloemer
1899	Sister M. Angela Leininger
1914	Sister Mary Joseph Dunn
1919	Sister Michelle Leininger
1920	Sister M. Denis Marcelle
1922	Sister M. Michelle Leininger
1923	Sister M. Angela Leininger
1929	Sister M. Mercedes O'Connell
1932	Sister M. Dolorosa Gough
1935	Sister M. Dominica Hettinger, Ph.D.
1938	Sister M. Casilda Bowling
1941	Sister M. Dolorosa Gough
1943	Sister M. Carmel Price
1950	Sister Mary Ruth Clemens
1951	Sister M. Theodolinda Obermeier
1958	Sister George Marie Long
1968	Sister Benedicta O'Connor
1970	Sister Jean Marie Hettinger
1972	Sister Eileen Carney
1973	Mr. James P. Clark
1975	Sister M. Laurana Burke
1978	Sister Louise Marie Willenbrink
1988	Sister M. Julienne Guy
1990	Sister Maureen Field, IHM
1994	Sister Paula Kleine-Kracht, Ph.D.
2001	Dr. Beverly McAuliffe

"What I love about SHA and have loved for many years is that Sacred Heart Academy is such a caring community of colleagues, students and parents."

—Sister Louise Marie Willenbrink '52
Principal, 1978-1988

Sister Sarah Stauble, Music, 1958

*"Sacred Heart's same gender
education empowers women.
I remember Father C.J. Wagner,
with much fear and respect....
He instilled in me a desire to be
prepared and to become an orator.
Shakespeare continues to be a
favorite of mine because of
Father Wagner. I would love to
return to SHA, and I'm very
comforted that my daughter will
someday attend Sacred Heart."*

—Judge Judith McDonald Burkman '77
Circuit Court Judge, Jefferson County

Father C.J. Wagner, English

Sister Helen O'Brien '53, History

"The Ursuline idea of 'sharing' has always been instilled in me, beginning with my education in elementary school. We train our students to become loving, Christian women who practice the four ideals of community, reverence, leadership and service. I feel that SHA provides the best education for girls in the city of Louisville."

—Mary Ann Kollros
Foreign language,
1964-present

"SHA is home to me, and has been for most of my life. My next hope is for a Sacred Heart Academy graduate to become an astronaut...."

—Sister Lorna Weiler '58
Science, chemistry and physics teacher at SHA for 35 years.
Beaker, the poodle, was a gift from her students in 1984.

Above: Carrie Morrison, Director of Marketing, Ursuline Campus Schools, and Fran Gallalee Peters '89, Campus Minister

Right: Angela Lincoln, Religion

Opposite page: Dr. Dan Van Meter, foreign language, receives the Loretta P. Mudd Excellence in Teaching Award

"My father chose Sacred Heart for me when I was a student because he heard it was the best. I joined the Ursulines and though I have been other places, this is where I was meant to be."

—Sr. Judith Rice '62
    English teacher, 1968-73;
    1999-present
    SHA Dean of Studies 1979-1998

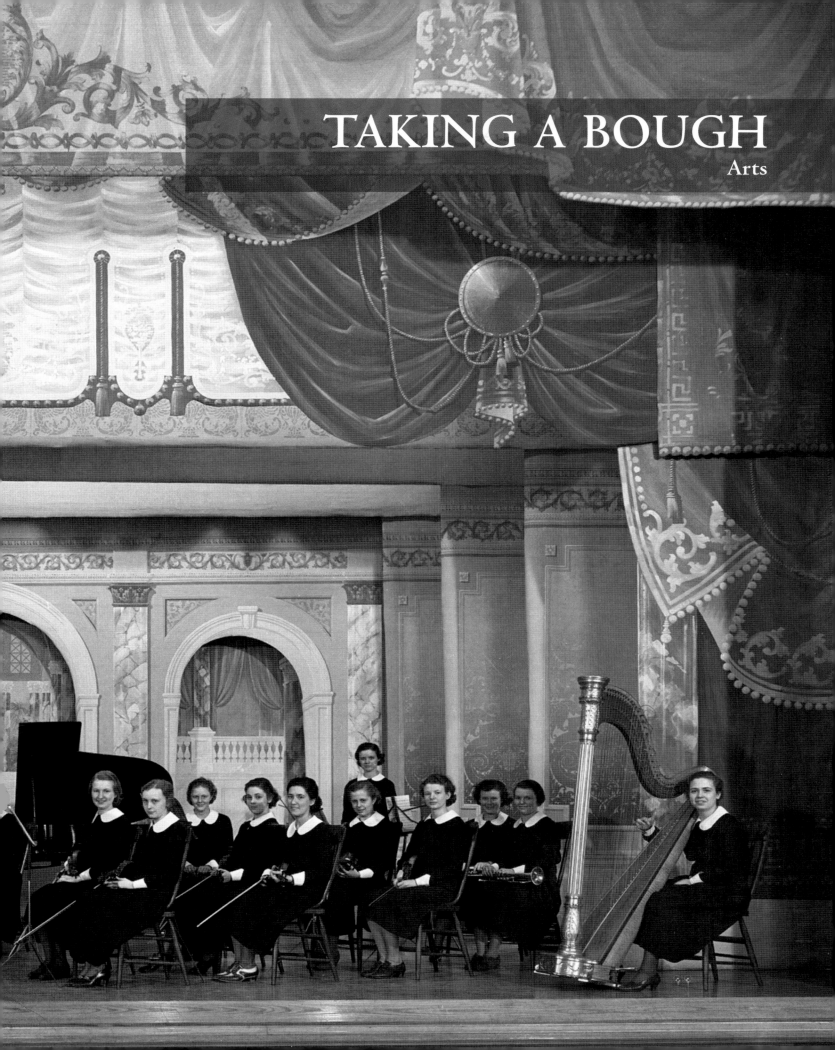

TAKING A BOUGH

Arts

Your daughters sing, while vistas ring

The memories are legion: an awkward freshman ballet class, a first published poem on a page in *Tapers*, a stirring A Cappella concert under the direction of Sister Ida Jones, a life-changing encounter with a Shakespearean comedy, a pointillist painting, a medieval melody, a post-modernist novel, a classic tour jeté.

The arts have been an integral part of daily life at Sacred Heart Academy from its earliest years. One of the first visual-art classes was a workshop in landscape sketching, an art form for which the Lexington Road campus and its nearby parks provided plenty of inspiration.

Music, too, has long been a vital element of the extra-curricular life of the school, with Sister Ida leading the way with her founding and directing of choirs from 1930 through 1969.

It may be that Sacred Heart's insistence on exposing students to the fine arts grew out of the European cultural background of the Ursulines. Or perhaps it was a natural component for a girls' boarding school at the turn of the 20th century.

Whatever the reason for its strong presence in the curriculum, Sacred Heart grads have benefited from its rewards for more than a century. As early as 1883, Sacred Heart students were sharing their creative endeavors with the community at large through public performances.

It's not surprising then, that the Academy's alumnae have made their mark in a wide array of artistic genres. These include writers, vocalists, dancers, painters, jewelry makers and graphic designers, to mention just a few. Today the tradition is stronger than ever, with the addition of SHA's art, media and technology wing, which offers an art studio and gallery showplace, photography dark rooms, a kiln and pottery area, as well as equipment for graphic design, videography, animation and web design. In recent years, the vocal arts department and the A Cappella choir have continued to bring recognition and honor to Sacred Heart, a tribute to the wisdom and farsightedness of the academy's founding sisters.
—*Dianne Aprile '67*

Avis (Sister Ida) Jones
as student, 1916

Opposite page: Sister Ida
as a teacher at SHA

Pages 194-195:
Orchestra, 1934

Orchestra, 1911

Dance class, 1934

Poetry Club, 1943

Mimi Wathen Dingman '57
Art and ballet teacher, SHA

A Cappella Choir, conducted by
Irma Dell Smith Von Barkhausen

"I had a dream in music that was always encouraged by SHA. Mrs. Jean Cassady realized once that I'd taken all the courses in music SHA offered, so she added a new class. I have many things to be thankful for from Sacred Heart, but the thing that strikes me the most is the idea that you can be anything you desire."

—Kim Greenwell Kahan '81
International Opera Singer

A Cappella Choir,
Mrs. Jean Cassady conducting

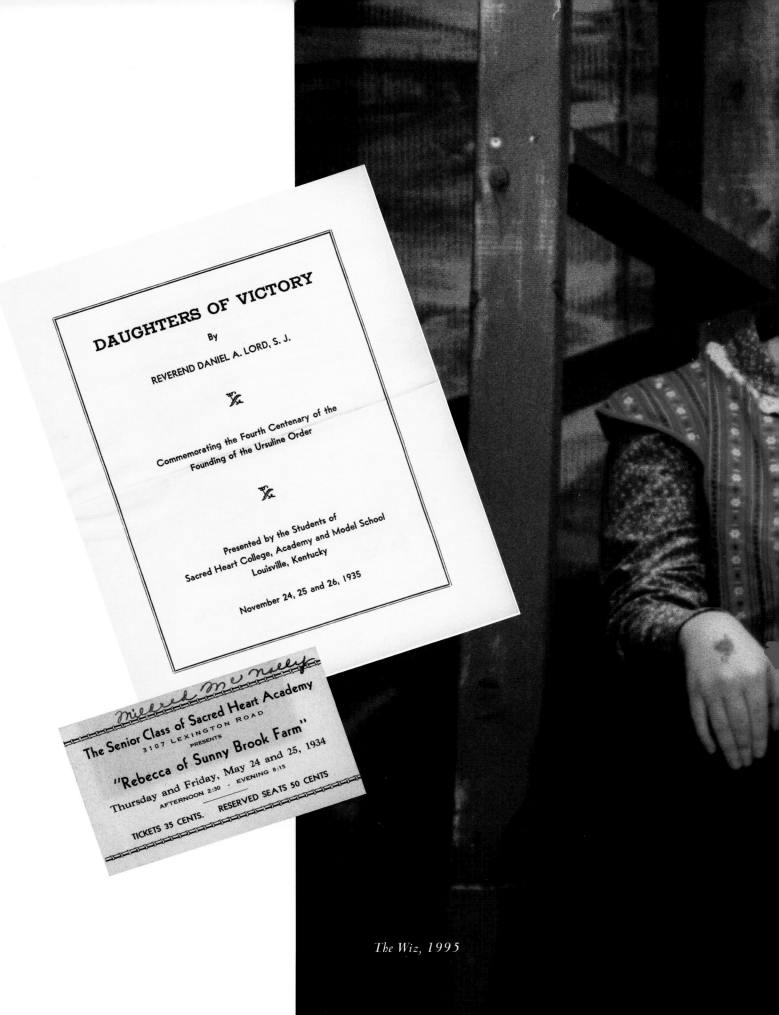

DAUGHTERS OF VICTORY

By

REVEREND DANIEL A. LORD, S. J.

Commemorating the Fourth Centenary of the
Founding of the Ursuline Order

Presented by the Students of
Sacred Heart College, Academy and Model School
Louisville, Kentucky

November 24, 25 and 26, 1935

Mildred McNeely

The Senior Class of Sacred Heart Academy
3107 LEXINGTON ROAD
PRESENTS
"Rebecca of Sunny Brook Farm"
Thursday and Friday, May 24 and 25, 1934
AFTERNOON 2:30 — EVENING 8:15

TICKETS 35 CENTS.   RESERVED SEATS 50 CENTS

The Wiz, 1995

Like many talented SHA students, Erin Brady Worsham '76 graduated with high hopes. Her world crashed around her in 1994, when she was diagnosed with the debilitating and often fatal ALS— Lou Gehrig's disease. Erin is confined to a wheelchair and is linked to a ventilator and feeding tube, but still spends her day creating art like the poster at right, using the "Liberator," a computer which allows her to create computer generated art by twitching her eyebrow. Her art has been exhibited nationally.

"Our Ursuline Sisters gave us a solid foundation to cope with the outside world and become happy, productive citizens. Giving back to the students of Sacred Heart is the best investment I ever made."

—Frances Dueser Steber '37
Patron of "Studio 37" in SHA's
Art, Media and Technology wing

Above: A Cappella, 2002

Opposite page: Madrigal Choir, 2002

A Cappella wins Esprit De Corps Award, 2002

PRESSED FLOWERS

Traditions

PRESSED FLOWERS

Traditions

Setting the hearth fires and tapers aglow

Big Sisters. Senior Prom. Graduation Mass. Hockey Games at Seneca Park. May Processions. Student Council Campaigns. Hootenannies. Basketball Tournaments. Ballet Recitals. Yearbook Signatures. Roses. Caps and Gowns. Father-Daughter Dances.

What is high school without its rituals? What are fond memories without ceremonies to commemorate them? What is a rich, nurturing Academy history without cherished traditions and practices passed down from class to class? Sacred Heart grew from the seeds of a proud heritage of Ursuline ideals and actions, and gradually generated its own unique customs and traditions. Today's rituals reflect a far different world from the one that existed 125 years ago. Even so, they represent the same respect for the past and the same strong ties to the values of the school's founders, as those described by Father Daniel Lord in the school song he wrote over 50 years ago:

"Loving you so, onward we go,
Setting the hearth fires and tapers aglow.
Fling we our colors to brighten the sky,
Daring to try, hearts beating high;
We shall remember and love you,
We vow, ever as now, dear Sacred Heart."
School song by Fr. Daniel Lord, SJ

—Dianne Aprile '67

Dance, 1948

*Opposite page: Field Day
Student Council patch,
1952, dance card, 1950
and class ring, 1979*

OF THE

HEART

Louisville, Kentucky.

ee Imshoff _____ has

_____ Course of Study, as prescribed

in scholarship and integrity of

and is therefore entitled to this

MA

Words and Music by

Fr. Daniel Lord, SJ was a nationally known author, playwright, musician, composer, lecturer and youth leader. He made frequent visits to SHA from 1925 to 1954, beginning with a joint retreat in 1925 for SHA and Ursuline Academy students. He is most fondly remembered on the Ursuline Campus as the composer of the alma mater songs for Ursuline College and Sacred Heart Academy. To this day, his music fills the halls of SHA and is featured at every graduation ceremony.

Graduation, 1931

222

AUTOGRAPHS

"Love and fear God."
Sister M. Augustine
Sacred Heart Academy.
July 3, 1893.

The Girl Graduate's
Memory Book

SHA

Odds and
~~Scores~~

Seniors of '25 visit[ed]
Alamo Theatre to [see]
"Inferno" Nov 6, 1[924]

Feb 23, 1925 Ann[...]
over and we ha[d ...]
of fun.

We spent [...]
at Laura's home, [...]
We visited the haunted [...]
most beautiful flowers & ate [...]

never after.
Edith's surprise
party
Mah 19

Social Events

'Mid music and laughter,
Light hearted and free,
With Youth ever after,
How joyous are we.

The Freshmen entertained the High School with an enjoyable evening. The refreshments were delicious.

To My Valentine

Lucille Blake

SACRED HEART ACADEMY
Halloween Mixer
Friday, October 31
9:00pm

Beach Party
music by
Nervous Melvin
Friday, Jan 13, 1989

Beach Party
SHA Gym
Friday January 15th,
9 p.m. to

"MY GIRL"
FATHER DAUGHTER DANCE
SHA
Saturday

Daddy's Lit

Be The
BEAT!
SHA
88-89

100 CLUB
SHA
66-67

UPSET
URSULINE

SHA

...TIL THEY
COME HOME

Now you can
"Be A Part of it All"
Student Activities Card
$2.50 — Good for 20 chances
Name: _____ Hr: _____
1985-1986 Student Council

DESERT STORM
I SUPPORT
OUR BOYS

OUT OF UNIFORM
Please admit _____
Reason { Satisfactory / Unsatisfactory }
Sister George Marie
Principal
No. 21   The Lamberty Co., Inc., Chicago

Form 75C
DETENTION SLIP
Date _____ Last Name _____
Reason _____ 19 ___ First Name _____
Room _____

Mother-Daughter Tea, 1940s

Junior Prom, 1947

Class of 1948 reunion

"I cannot imagine a greater job than being the Alumnae Director for Sacred Heart Academy. I love coming to work every day because it is a constant reminder of all the wonderful experiences and friendships I enjoyed when I attended Sacred Heart. It is such a joy to see the great traditions still being played out in the classrooms and all the activities and even a greater joy seeing the generations of women who are so connected to this campus."

—Nannette Mershon '67

During World War I, Sacred Heart began holding its Senior Prom in December rather than in the traditional month of May. The change was made to accommodate the times: the Christmas holidays were a time when servicemen were more likely to be home on leave and available for dates. After the war, the Prom returned to May—until World War II, when it was moved back to December. It has remained a holiday tradition to this day.

Senior Snow Ball (Prom), 1950

Senior Prom, 1955

Senior Prom, 1959

Valentine Dance, 1969

Father-Daughter Dance

Dance, 1974

Freshman-Sophomore Dance

238

"Sacred Heart girls of all ages share a common bond and a special sisterhood. We are everywhere, and we're always there for each other. Many of my closest friends and co-workers today are women who graduated from Sacred Heart."

—Carol Kunk Butler '68
Attorney, Project and
Event Director

Junior Ring Ceremony

Graduates, 1997

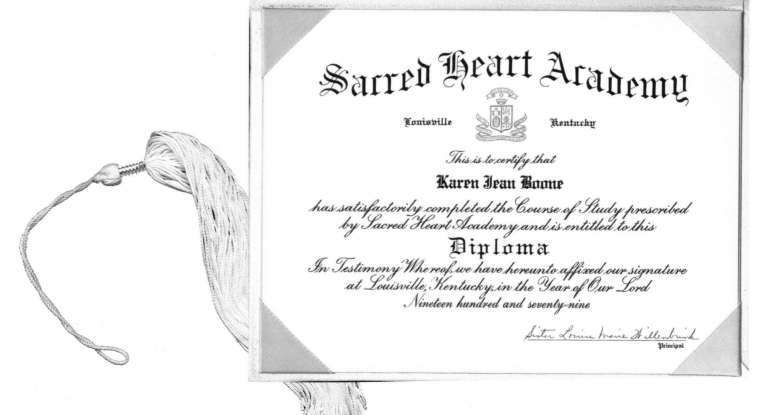

Sacred Heart Academy

Louisville   Kentucky

This is to certify that

Karen Jean Boone

has satisfactorily completed the Course of Study prescribed by Sacred Heart Academy and is entitled to this

Diploma

In Testimony Whereof, we have hereunto affixed our signature at Louisville, Kentucky, in the Year of Our Lord Nineteen hundred and seventy-nine

Sister Louise Marie Willenbrink
Principal

Graduation, 2002

Faculty at Graduation, 2002

244

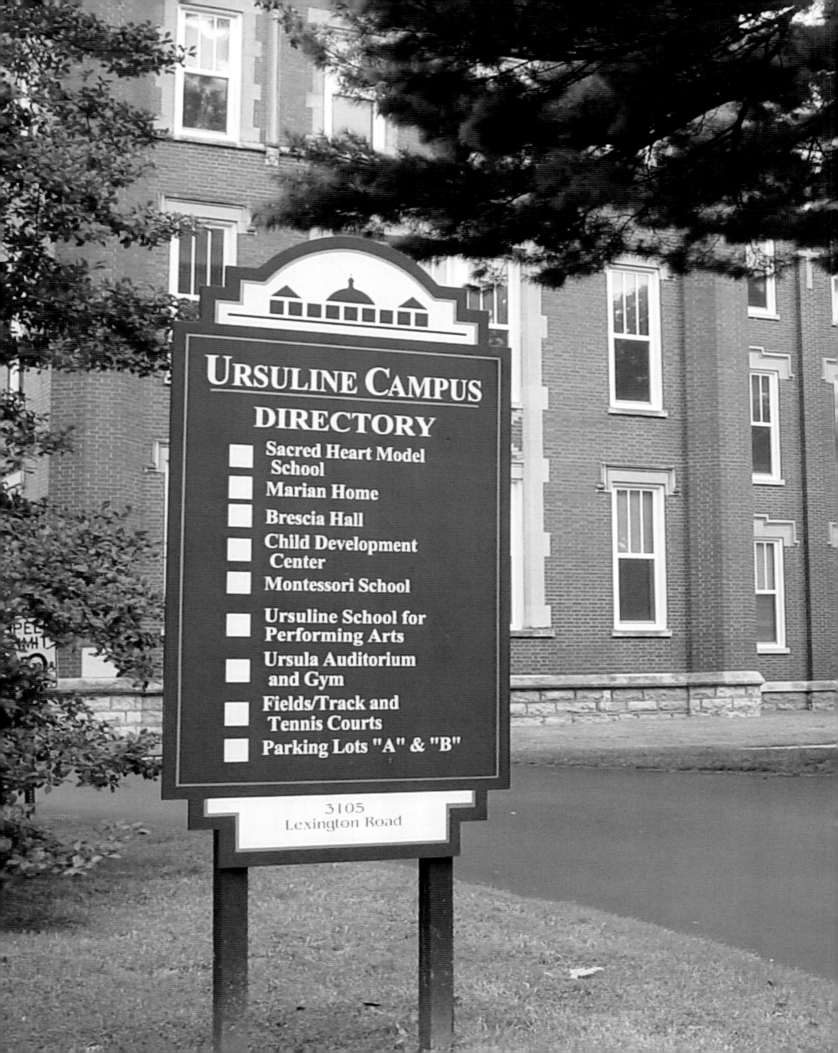

URSULINE CAMPUS
DIRECTORY

- Sacred Heart Model School
- Marian Home
- Brescia Hall
- Child Development Center
- Montessori School

- Ursuline School for Performing Arts
- Ursula Auditorium and Gym
- Fields/Track and Tennis Courts
- Parking Lots "A" & "B"

3105
Lexington Road

HEARTY BRANCHES
Other Campus Schools

HEARTY BRANCHES

Other Campus Schools

Fling we our colors to brighten the sky

Sacred Heart Academy and the campus surrounding it have always been about growth, progress and expansion. Growth of spirit and mind. Progress in education at all levels. Expansion of goals, dreams, ideals, boundaries, services.

And so, it was natural that out of the original dream that gave birth to Sacred Heart Academy, other schools and youth-oriented programs would grow. Over time, "Ursuline Campus," as it became known, evolved to include a model school, Montessori school, performing arts school, child care center and a college that later moved to another site. As needs changed, so did the campus and its services.

On June 26, 1990, the Ursuline Sisters took a bold step into the future. They separately incorporated and joined the five institutions still thriving on campus to form Ursuline Campus Schools, Inc.

Sisters and community leaders now function as a board of trustees.

In each stage of their history, the Ursuline Sisters of Louisville have responded generously to the demands of the times, as their founder, Saint Angela Merici counseled centuries ago. Angela's ideals, combined with the values of the Bavarian sisters who came to Louisville in 1858, live on in the principles of each of the Ursuline Campus Schools.

From the seeds of Sacred Heart Academy, planted 125 years ago, the Ursuline philosophy has branched out and flourished.

—Dianne Aprile '67

Entrance to campus, 1950s

SACRED HEART
MODEL SCHOOL

Sacred Heart Model School (grades one through eight) was formed from SHA in 1924. It began in the manor house on the original 10 3/8 acres purchased by the sisters in 1877.

By the early 1950s that building was both too small and unsuitable for elementary school children. Parents worked with the Ursuline Sisters to build, on the east end of the campus, a three-story structure that became known as Angela Hall. The cornerstone was laid on May 27, 1955. Through the years the Model School held classes in Ursula Hall, Brescia Hall and Angela Hall. In 1999, it moved to the 1924 building that once housed Sacred Heart Academy.

Sacred Heart Model School traditionally has been coeducational, except for a brief period in the late 1950s. In the beginning, boys were enrolled only through sixth grade; however, since 1969 the school has been co-ed for kindergarten through eighth grade.

The program has received numerous awards and its students excel in competitions, both citywide and statewide. In 2001, with Dr. Sarah Wannemuehler as principal, the school was recognized by the United States Department of Education as a Blue Ribbon School of Excellence.

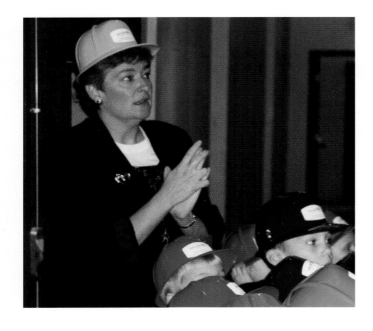

Sacred Heart Model School

Left: Dr. Sarah Wannemuehler, Principal, SHMS

Walt Ecker '27 was the only male student in his class at Sacred Heart Model School in 1932. Ecker, in fact, made history the following year—as the school's first male graduate. Male students traditionally left the Model School in seventh grade to finish at parish schools. But in his wake, three male students in the class behind his also stayed on, and soon male graduates were the norm.

SACRED HEART JUNIOR COLLEGE/ URSULINE COLLEGE

Sacred Heart Junior College (SHJC) opened in 1921 as a two-year program primarily to educate Ursuline Sisters for the many parochial schools opening across the country. It moved into Ursula Hall in 1925. In 1938, renamed Ursuline College, it began offering four-year baccalaureate programs. In 1940, Sister Angela Van Natta became dean, and Brescia Hall became the new home for the College.

The post-secondary programs on the Ursuline Campus always had both boarding and day students. Marian Hall was completed in 1955 as a college dorm and also contained a chapel, library, dining room and some college offices. In 1977, the building was renovated to meet requirements for a Kentucky licensed nursing facility for Ursuline Sisters. The college opened a second dorm, Julianne Hall, in 1962. This building was originally Woodcock Hall, an Episcopalian orphanage for boys. Shortly after the purchase, a four-story dormitory wing was added. In 1998, Julianne Hall was razed to accommodate a parking lot for Sacred Heart Academy.

In 1968, Ursuline College and Bellarmine College, which was all male at the time, merged to become Bellarmine-Ursuline College. All college classes moved to the Bellarmine campus, and later the name was changed to Bellarmine University.

OTHER PROGRAMS

In 1956 Sister Raymond Carter, dean of Ursuline College, Sister Jane Frances Baumann and Mary Ann Fueglein established a program that grew into the WHAS-TV Crusade for Children Speech Clinic.

For 40 years, the Clinic provided therapy for speech and language disorders and until 1968, training for clinicians. The Speech Clinic closed in 1996.

The Ursuline Education Center for children with learning disabilities opened in 1964 in Ursula Hall under the direction of Sister Mary Vincent Strittmatter. This program, established by Ursuline College, merged with the Msgr. Pitt Learning Center in 1981.

Ursuline sisters also operated the Ursuline Tutoring Center from 1976 to 1990. Since that time, sisters tutor individuals when requested.

Sister Mary Odilla Gadlage with special needs children

Sister Stephen Disselkamp

URSULINE MONTESSORI SCHOOL

The Ursuline Montessori School opened in 1967 under the leadership of Sister Marlene Oetken. The program provides an environment which allows children to develop intellectual, physical and psychological abilities. While initial efforts revolved around early childhood education, in 1997 the program expanded to include a Montessori elementary school for children in levels one through three.

In 1999, the school grew to welcome fourth and fifth graders, and in 2000 the preschool program began accepting two-year-olds. The Ursuline Montessori School continues to enjoy success today, with ground broken in the spring of 2002 for a new, state-of-the-art school building.

Linda Otto (middle) director of Ursuline Montessori School at the groundbreaking for new pre-school facilities, 2002

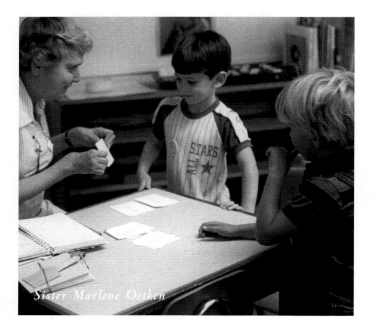

Sister Marlene Oetken

URSULINE CHILD DEVELOPMENT CENTER

In 1986, the Ursuline Board of Directors recognized the need to provide additional child care for parents with children in Sacred Heart Model School or in the Ursuline Montessori School. The one-story building behind the Ursuline Motherhouse was remodeled to accommodate a before and after school center and was approved by the Kentucky Cabinet of Human Resources. During the first year, under the direction of Sister Vera Del Grande, the Center's license was extended to a full day care center, and it was renamed the Ursuline Child Development Center (UCDC). In July 1989, UCDC moved into a new facility at the north end of Ursuline Campus.

*Mrs. Vicki Furlow,
director, Ursuline Child
Development Center*

*Opposite page bottom:
Sister Vera Del Grande*

URSULINE
SCHOOL FOR THE
PERFORMING ARTS

In 1968, the Ursuline School of Music opened, led by Sister Serena Stauble. In 1977, a drama program was introduced and the school's title changed to the Ursuline School of Music and Drama.

Since 1998, dance has also become an important segment of the school. Reflecting this wide variety of arts education for children as well as adults, the school is now known as the Ursuline School for the Performing Arts.

Sound of Music, 1983

Performing Arts Director Anna Jo Paul with cast from the Wiz

In 2002, Orson and Kathy Oliver made a $100,000 gift to the Ursuline School for the Performing Arts in memory of their daughter Jana, who passed away at the age of 19 in 1995.

The Jana Oliver Endowment Fund honors the Olivers' daughter, who studied for 16 years at four of the five schools on the Ursuline Campus. It will help offset the substantial annual costs of student productions at USPA.

Jesus Christ Superstar, 2002

266

Sacred Heart Model School art show, 2002

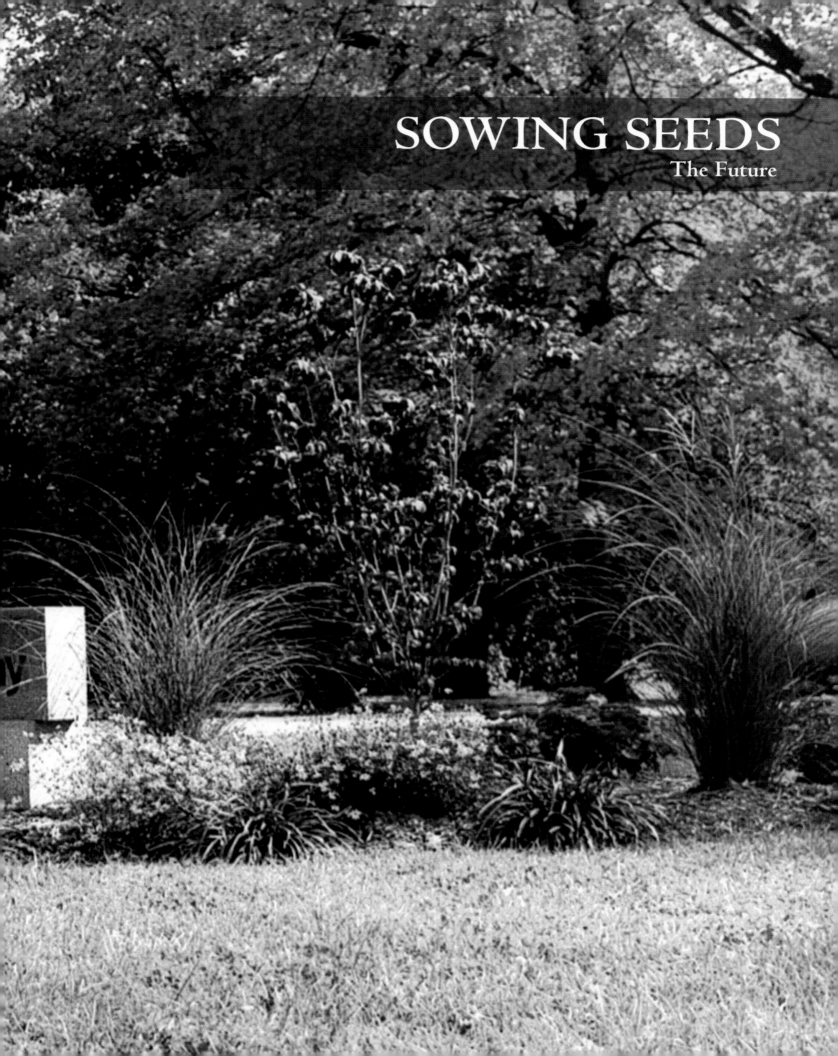

SOWING SEEDS

The Future

SOWING SEEDS

The Future

by Dr. Beverly McAuliffe
Principal, Sacred Heart Academy

Loving you so, onward we go

My vision for SHA is a Catholic high school filled with bright girls who eagerly embrace the Ursuline core values of community, leadership, reverence and service, and with faculty and staff who model those values each and every day for their students.

I am very fortunate to have on the faculty a former SHA principal, Sister Louise Marie Willenbrink, who is now the senior counselor, and Sister Judith Rice and Ann Cunningham, both of whom are former SHA assistant principals. All three are SHA alumnae as well. I trust their advice and have relied on it frequently. They have been in my shoes at SHA, and I respect their guidance.

I am also grateful to have a number of faculty members who have been at SHA for many years. SHA has teachers and staff members like Mary Ann Kollros, Sheila Huff, Sister Lorna Weiler and Sister Annalita Fox who are truly devoted to SHA and are always willing to grow and change for the good of the students, keeping me connected to SHA's past as we help to plan for its future.

I envision more diversity in the school, both adults and students. Students will be more aware of global issues and will be challenged to be catalysts for societal changes that bring peace and justice.

The focus on community service will continue to grow as we challenge our students to be leaders and doers, as well as life-long learners who search for truth while recognizing that God is the source of all truth.

I see continuing technological improvements and curricular additions to address the rapidly changing world that students will find beyond high school. The school building will continue to be updated with a remodeled front office and a new counseling suite, renovated science labs, a new heating and air-conditioning system, new windows and improved classroom lighting.

Sacred Heart will continue to excel in sports. As talented coaches guide our outstanding sports program, the success of our athletes will continue. Our athletes will win championships in sports like lacrosse, ice hockey and crew, as well as volleyball, basketball, soccer and swimming.

Being principal of a school bathed in so much history is wonderful. I love being at Sacred Heart! Each day is a joy, even the hardest ones. I am very fortunate to be able to spend my days with the students who give me energy and keep me invigorated. It is a privilege to be Sacred Heart Academy's principal.

274

Life's Journey

by Charles Francesconi
President, Ursuline Campus Schools

Life's journey takes us on unexpected travels, on paths for which we hadn't planned, to destinations we never anticipated. Ten years ago my life's journey took me to the Ursuline Campus to serve on its Board of Trustees. What followed shortly thereafter—a new career as President of Ursuline Campus Schools—was indeed an unexpected turn in my life's journey, a path and destination I had not planned for nor anticipated.

My role as president is to help build a first-rate vision for each of the schools and for the campus as a whole, then give direction and obtain resources to help achieve that vision. That vision is formed from the fortunate combination of a strong foundation, the values, tradition, and educational experience of the Ursuline Sisters, and the framework of our mission to educate the whole person. The task is not without challenges and occasional disappointments, but when surrounded by gifted educators, concerned parents and generous alums, the task becomes more easily achievable.

We strive to preserve the quality of an Ursuline education, retain the values of community, leadership, reverence and service and deliver the best service to our students in the context of their current environment. It's a dynamic process because the student environment is constantly changing at a faster pace than ever before. The vision has many facets including the most current and appropriate curriculum, suitable facilities, athletic and artistic challenges and opportunities to serve others in our community.

Bringing this vision closer to reality has made this unexpected path and destination of my life's journey more fulfilling than I could ever have imagined. I give thanks to the entire Ursuline Campus community for making this possible.

Left to right: Beverly McAuliffe, principal, Sacred Heart Academy; Charles Francesconi, president, Ursuline Campus Schools; Sister Sarah Stauble, immediate past president, Ursuline Sisters; Mindi Rummel, dean of studies, Sacred Heart Academy; Mike Hardesty, dean of students, Sacred Heart Academy; Sister Louise Marie Willenbrink, counselor, Sacred Heart Academy.

An Ursuline Perspective

by Sister Jean Anne Zappa
President, Ursuline Sisters

Being a part of the Ursuline Campus is much more than new building projects or the expansion of programs. And, it is more than academic achievements. We continually strive to accomplish these successes in the context of a rich heritage of Catholic/Ursuline tradition.

Each of us who comes to this campus is challenged to absorb the Ursuline values and heritage. We are called to motivate and to model for one another the mission, values and legacy that the Ursuline Sisters have shared with the campus family. We are called to be good stewards; we have been entrusted with a sacred gift of ensuring the teaching mission of Jesus.

My hope and vision is that all who are connected with Sacred Heart Academy and the other Ursuline Campus schools—trustees, parents, teachers, staff, administrators, students, Ursulines and all who visit here—will catch the spirit of Saint Angela as she lived and expressed her relationship with God "to be glory to the only God" and to serve the needs of others. May we embrace that spirit and live and share it with each other.

"Having now graduated from SHA, I realize how lucky I was to attend such an all-around amazing school. I will forever be thankful for the love and support I received in those four years. Sacred Heart was always 100% supportive of who I am and of the advocacy work I do."

—Deanna Durrett '00
National anti-tobacco advocate

"I love being a freshman at SHA. It is great to be one of the youngest parts of such an old tradition. I will always look back on my days at SHA and smile, because I know high school will be one of the most fun-filled, exciting times of my life. The name fits the school perfectly— Sacred Heart Academy really does have HEART!"

—Carson Massler, SHA '05

ACKNOWLEDGMENTS

Special thanks to the following alumnae and friends of Sacred Heart Academy who donated some of the items and information used in this commemorative book:

Archives of the Ursuline Sisters
Carol Boone '51
Penny Cooper Burns '61
Bill and Carol Kunk Butler '68
Kim Cochrane '97
Judy Condon '64
The Courier-Journal, Michael Clevenger
Jeannie Lechleiter Donovan '86
Walter Ecker
Randell Elkins Photography
Jane Miranda Elpers '55
Sr. Dorothy Frankrone '41
Joyce Young Guetig, UA '51
Becky Sisco Guthrie '58
Joan Wagner Hammer '45
Dorothy Greweling Kellner '34
Dean Lavenson Photography
Colleen Herbig Magruder '60
Sharon Allgaier Magruder '60
Mary Ann Mitchell '55
Pat Moran '54
Carrie A. Morrison
Anne Gottbrath Padon '67
Patrick Pfister Photography
Anna Lee Porter '42
Carolyn Reed '77
Michelle Resch '70
Kristen Steudle '87
Kathy Trompeter '75
University of Louisville Photographic Archives
Chris Vale Photography
Nanette Merkley Vale '86

And grateful thanks to the following Ursuline Sisters, whose research and publications were essential resources for this book:

Sister Rosamond Besendorf '35
Sister Martha Buser '49
Sister Mary deLourdes Gohmann
Sister Pat Lowman
Sister Irene Mahoney
Sister Helen Margaret Schweri '29

The Book Committee

Book Design: Karen Boone '79
Executive Editor: Laura Guetig '86
Historical Text and Chapter Introductions: Dianne Aprile '67
Historical Research and Editing: Sister Martha Jacob '53

Dianne Aprile '67 is a former staff writer and columnist for *The Courier-Journal* and *Louisville Times*. She is the author of four books and currently is book columnist for *Louisville Magazine*. She is a member of the graduate school faculty of Spalding University, where she teaches creative non-fiction.

Karen Boone '79 has designed many books, including *Keeneland—Reflections on a Thoroughbred Tradition*. She has designed two official Kentucky Derby Festival posters. She received her post graduate degree from the School of Design in Basel, Switzerland, and worked for Pentagram Design in New York, San Francisco, and for PAOS in Tokyo, Japan.

Carol Kunk Butler '68 is a lawyer who presently serves as a Special Assistant to the President and Director of Special Projects and Events for the University of Louisville. She and her husband Bill own a local book publishing company, Butler Books, and she is a member of the Board of Trustees of Ursuline Campus Schools.

Laura Guetig '86 is an award-winning writer and video producer for Kentucky's largest independent public relations firm. She is also the author of a mystery series, written under the pen name of Laura Young.

Sister Martha Jacob '53 has been an Ursuline Sister for 40 years. She has taught at Ursuline College and five other universities, and has served as Director of Development and/or Communications for the Ursuline Sisters for 20 years. She is currently the archivist for the Ursuline Sisters.

Sister Colette Kraemer '50 has been an Ursuline Sister for 52 years. She taught four years at Sacred Heart Model School and nine years at Sacred Heart Academy. She currently serves as Director of Mission Effectiveness for Ursuline Campus Schools and is a member of the Board of Trustees of Ursuline Campus Schools.

Nannette Mershon '67 is Alumnae Director and Associate Director of Development for Sacred Heart Academy.

Gathering 125 years of history is a challenging and rewarding task. While every effort has been made to verify facts, names and dates, we apologize for any unintentional errors.

Sacred Heart ♥ Academy

Sacred Heart Academy
3175 Lexington Road
Louisville KY 40206
(502) 897-6097
www.sacredheartacad.com

URSULINE CAMPUS SCHOOLS

Ursuline Campus Schools
3105 Lexington Road
Louisville KY 40206
(502) 896-3910
www.ucschools.com

URSULINE SISTERS
OF LOUISVILLE

CONTINUING THE LEGACY OF
SPIRITUALITY AND SERVICE

Ursuline Sisters of Louisville
3105 Lexington Road
Louisville KY 40206
(502) 897-1811
www.ursulineslou.org

SACRED HEART ACADEMY'S PLACE IN HISTORY: 1877-2002

1875   **1880**   **1885**   **1890**

At Sacred Heart

1877: Ursuline Sisters buy ten acres on Shelbyville Branch Turnpike (now Lexington Road) and open Academy of the Sacred Heart.

1879: Boarders are admitted to SHA, and the original building gets an addition to accommodate the new students.

1887: Ursuline Academy becomes a day school; its boarders are sent to SHA.

1888: First commencement; SHA graduates its first student, Miss Sabina Orrick of Canton, Mississippi; first First Communion at SHA.

In Louisville

Aristides

1875: The First Kentucky Derby runs at Churchill Downs.

1882: The Southern Exposition opens in Louisville.

1889: Louisville opens its first line of electric trolley cars, triggering a real-estate boom.

Around the Country

1876: Gen. Custer dies at Little Big Horn.

1877: Presidential election settled in favor of Rutherford Hayes by one electoral vote.

1878: Southern states are free of federal troops for the first time since the Civil War ended.

1882: President James Garfield is killed by an assassin and is succeeded by Chester A. Arthur.

1884: Grover Cleveland elected President.

1888: Benjamin Harrison becomes President, defeating Grover Cleveland.

At Sacred Heart

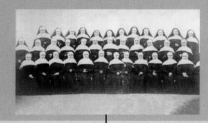
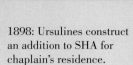

1894: Ursuline Sisters move their novitiate from Shelby Street to SHA campus.

1898: Ursulines construct an addition to SHA for chaplain's residence.

1904: A new SHA, designed by architect C. A. Curtin, opens for occupancy.

1905: SHA Alumnae Association is established.

In Louisville

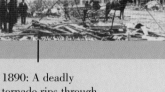

1890: A deadly tornado rips through Louisville, causing $2 million in damage and killing 100 people.

1902: First automobile in Louisville.

1905: Seelbach Hotel opens at Fourth and Walnut.

1907: A new capitol opens in Frankfort. Louisville gives up dream of being state capital.

Around the Country

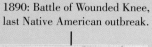

1890: Battle of Wounded Knee, last Native American outbreak.

1898: Spanish-American War fought in Cuba and the Philippines.

1901: President McKinley is killed; Theodore Roosevelt succeeds him.

1903: The Wright Brothers make aviation history at Kitty Hawk, N.C.

1910: SHA adopts a school song: *Dear SHA*, by L.M. Kemper and A.L. Morgan. Later, that song is replaced by *Dear Sacred Heart* by Rev. Daniel A. Lord, S.J.

1917: New Ursuline Motherhouse is dedicated.

1918: Fire destroys SHA building, causing an estimated loss of $200,000.

1924: Cornerstone is laid for a new SHA to replace the one destroyed by fire.

1912: The Majestic Theater opens.

1918: Robert Worth Bingham buys *The Courier-Journal*, located then at Third and Liberty.

1922: WHAS, Louisville's first radio station, begins broadcasting.

1923: 15-story Brown Hotel opens at Fourth and Broadway.

Jim Walton on WHAS's "Coffee Call."

1912: Woodrow Wilson elected President.

1914: World War I begins.

1920: Prohibition becomes law: the nation becomes officially "dry."

1923: Warren Harding dies; Calvin Coolidge sworn in as President

1924: Calvin Coolidge elected President.

1925   **1935**   **1940**   **1945**

At Sacred Heart

1925: Ursula Hall is built for Sacred Heart Junior College.

1931: Annual tuition and room and board at SHA is $435.

1938: Sacred Heart Junior College expanded and renamed Ursuline College.

1940: Sacred Heart stops taking boarding students.

In Louisville

 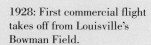 

1927: The J. B. Speed Museum opens on the University of Louisville's Belknap Campus.

1928: First commercial flight takes off from Louisville's Bowman Field.

1937: The Great Ohio River Flood wreaks havoc in Louisville.

1941: Fort Knox begins training soldiers for a new level of armored warfare.

1942: Curtiss-Wright airplane plant etablished at Standiford Field.

Reclining Figure: Angles, by Henry Moore, at the Speed Museum.

Around the Country

1929: Stock market crashes; banks across the nation collapse.

1941: Japan makes surprise attack on Pearl Harbor; U.S. declares war.

1944: U.S. troops launch "D-Day" invasion of Normandy.

1945: Japan formally surrenders to the U.S.

"Black Thursday" in front of the New York Stock Exchange.

1955: Cornerstone laid for new Sacred Heart Model School.

1956: Senator John F. Kennedy visits SHA; the original home of SHA is torn down.

1962: Ground is broken for a new SHA building.
1963: The new SHA is completed, with convent attached.

1964: All SHA students are again in one building; Former SHA building becomes Administration Building for college.

1967: Ursuline Montessori School opens on Ursuline Campus.

1950: St. Matthews becomes an incorporated city; Bellarmine College (now University) opens.

1956: Kentucky Fair and Exposition Center opens.

1963: The Mall St. Matthews, Louisville's first enclosed shopping center, opens.

1965: 15-story Kaden Tower is built on Dutchman's Lane.

1950: Atomic bomb experimentation in the South Pacific.

1960: John F. Kennedy becomes the first (and only to date) Catholic President of the United States.

1962: Pope John XXIII convenes the Second Vatican Council.

1963: Martin Luther King Jr. gives his "I Have A Dream" speech in Washington, D.C.; John F. Kennedy assassinated.

1967: Thurgood Marshall becomes the first African-American Supreme Court justice.

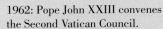

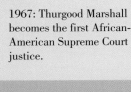

At Sacred Heart

1968: Ursuline School of Music (USPA) opens; SHA enrollment peaks at 952.

1972: An advisory board is formed to help SHA meet its $600,000 debt.

1974: The number of lay teachers exceeds the number of Ursuline Sisters at SHA for the first time.

1976: SHA wins state basketball championship; fire causes extensive damage to SHA's kitchen and cafeteria.

1977: SHA celebrates its 100th birthday, and makes its final payment on capital construction; new school sign donated by 1975-1978 classes.

In Louisville

1968: Louisville Zoological Gardens opens.

1974: Louisville is hit by major tornado on April 3.

1977: Museum of History and Science opens.

1980: Jefferson County's suburban population exceeds the city's for the first time.

Aerial view of Shelbyville Road at Oxmoor Center.

Around the Country

1968: Martin Luther King Jr. is assassinated in April; Robert F. Kennedy in June.

1969: Astronauts land on the moon in Apollo 11.

1974: President Richard Nixon resigns rather than be impeached over Watergate scandal.

1975: South Vietnam surrenders to North Vietnam; war is over for the U.S.

1980: Ronald Reagan elected president, defeating Jimmy Carter.

1981: SHA Alumnae Association presents its first Distinguished Alumna Award.

1984: SHA swimmer Mary T. Meagher '83 sets world records and wins three Olympic gold medals in swimming.
1986: UCDC (Ursuline Child Development Center) founded.

1987: Angeline Circle is established; SHA wins its 11th straight high school girls' golf championship.

1988: Mary Jane Herp honored for 40 years of teaching; SHA's first endowment drive is launched; goal is $1 million in five years.

1990: Ursuline Campus Schools, Inc. becomes a separate corporation, sponsored by the Ursulines; Valkyrie Hall of Fame for athletes is established.

1982-83: Galleria opens on Fourth Street, followed by the Kentucky Center for the Arts.

1986: Jerry Abramson takes office as Mayor of the City of Louisville.

1988: National headquarters of the Presbyterian Church (USA) moves to Louisville.

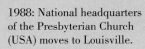

1981: President Reagan survives an assassination attempt; Sandra Day O'Connor becomes the first female member of the U.S. Supreme Court.

1983: Sally Ride becomes the first female U.S. astronaut.

1986: The space shuttle Challenger explodes.

1989: The Berlin Wall falls, as the Cold War ends.

1990: South Africa frees Nelson Mandela.

1990   **1995**   **2000**

At Sacred Heart

1991: SHA presents its first Heart Awards.

1995: Christmas toy drive for Appalachia is begun; The Interlude, a major fund-raiser for UCS, is initiated.

1998: Ground is broken for the $10 million campus renovation project; SHA is recognized as a Blue Ribbon National School of Excellence.

1999: The renovated Sacred Heart chapel is dedicated; new SHA gym, athletic fields, track and fieldhouse open.

2000: SHA's new Art and Technology wing opens.

2001: SHA wins state field hockey championship.

2002: SHA wins state basketball championship.

In Louisville

1990: Melissa Mershon '71 becomes first woman president of the Board of Aldermen.

1997: Anne Meagher Northup '66 becomes Representative of the Third Congressional District.

1998: Papa John's Cardinal Stadium opens in Louisville; The Vogue Theatre closes.

1999: David L. Armstrong becomes Mayor of Louisville; Rebecca Jackson becomes County-Judge Executive.

2000: Bellarmine University celebrates 50th anniversary; voters approve merger of city and county government.

Around the Country

  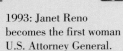  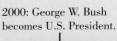  

1991: U.S. forces crush Iraq in the Persian Gulf War.

1993: Janet Reno becomes the first woman U.S. Attorney General.

1995: Bomb explodes at the Oklahoma City federal building, killing 168 people.

1999: Bill Clinton acquitted on articles of impeachment.

2000: George W. Bush becomes U.S. President.

2001: Terrorists attack New York City's World Trade Center and the Pentagon in Washington.

"Sacred Heart Academy's Place in History" was created by Sister Pat Lowman, O.S.U.

Sister Pat (formerly Sister Marcian) has been an Ursuline Sister for 62 years. She taught elementary school for 13 years in Kentucky, Nebraska and South Carolina. She was a beloved history teacher and chair of Social Studies at Sacred Heart Academy from 1958 to 1965. She was a professor of history at Ursuline College and Bellarmine University for 31 years, from 1965 to 1996.

While at Bellarmine, Sister Pat received the William T. Miles Memorial Award (1976) and a Distinguished Service Award from the Teacher Education Department (1990). She was voted "Teacher of the Year" by Bellarmine students four times. Bellarmine inaugurated a Sister Pat Lowman Award in 1996. In 2000 Sister Pat received an honorary doctorate from Bellarmine University and was inducted into its Athletic Hall of Fame.

Today she is a volunteer at Marian Home, and official scorer for the Bellarmine Women's basketball team.